THE COMPLETE
PAUL

THE COMPLETE

PAUL

A NEW ARRANGEMENT
of the APOSTLE'S WORDS

Douglas Wilson

canonpress
Moscow, Idaho

Published by Canon Press
P.O. Box 8729, Moscow, Idaho 83843
800.488.2034 | www.canonpress.com

Douglas Wilson, *The Complete Paul: A New Arrangement of the Apostle's Words*
Copyright ©2017 by Douglas Wilson

Cover design by James Engerbretson
Interior design by Valerie Anne Bost

Printed in the United States of America.

Library of Congress Cataloging-in-Publication Data:
Wilson, Douglas, 1953- author.
The complete Paul : a reader's edition / Douglas Wilson.
Moscow, Idaho : Canon Press, [2018]
LCCN 2018024496 | ISBN 9781947644021 (pbk. : alk. paper)
LCSH: Bible. Romans--Theology.
Classification: LCC BS2665.52 .W555 2018 | DDC 227/.05209--dc23
LC record available at https://lccn.loc.gov/2018024496

18 19 20 21 22 23 24   9 8 7 6 5 4 3 2 1

This book is in memory of Stephen,
deacon in the early church,
who, I am convinced,
was the principal human instrument
in preparing Saul of Tarsus
for his encounter with the risen Lord.

CONTENTS

INTRODUCTION

This book is intended to serve as a reader's edition to the words of the apostle Paul, as helpfully indicated by the title. If the quite familiar Paul can be made *fresh* as well as familiar, then the basic goal of this project will have been achieved. But a few words of explanation are still in order, as I did not simply assemble all of Paul's epistles in canonical order, stitching them together end-to-end. That would not be a bad thing in itself, but hardly worth publishing in a separate volume. That much could be obtained simply by reading Paul's letters in a particular order in your regular Bible. Instead, this is an involved collation of sorts.

Here is how this collation was done. I took the book of Romans to serve as the spine of this project, and then inserted passages from all his other epistles and portions of Acts in such a way as to fit within the structure of the book of Romans. It is a testimony to the greatness of *that* book that there was a natural place for pretty much every passage to go.

Many before me have noticed the characteristics of the book of Romans that would make it suitable for a project like this. Philip Melanchthon said Romans was the "compendium of all Christian doctrine,"[i] and structured his own first systematic work after the Apostle's.

Luther felt the same way: "This letter is truly the most important piece in the New Testament. It is purest Gospel . . . it seems that St. Paul, in writing this letter, wanted to compose a summary of the whole of Christian and evangelical teaching which would also be an introduction to the whole Old Testament."[ii] Frederic Godet memorably called it the "cathedral of Christian faith,"[iii] and Calvin considered it a "sure road" for understanding all the rest of Scripture.[iv] If anyone still doubts it is a worthy book to use in organizing all Paul's writings, then let Tyndale have the last word: "I think it meet that every Christian man not only know [Romans], by rote and without the book, but also exercise himself therein evermore continually, as with the daily bread of the soul. No man verily can read it too oft, or study it too well; for the more it is studied, the easier it is; the more it is chewed, the pleasanter it is."[v]

So when it comes to understanding Paul, Romans is *the* book to master. And to return to Godet's image of a cathedral, what I have done is taken the magnificent structure of that great cathedral, and have fashioned all the stained glass windows out of his other words from all his other epistles.

In other words, this is a collation of all the words that are reliably *attributed* to the apostle Paul by Scripture. Framing the project in this way solves the problem of the book of Hebrews, which I take as Pauline in some important sense, but which other believing scholars don't.

But in any case, no explicit statement in Scripture is made about the authorship of that particular book, and so I felt free to treat it as *unattributed* to Paul. But all the other epistles, unbelieving scholarship notwithstanding, are attributed to Paul by the words of Scripture itself, and this means that, for faithful believers, all those books must be accepted as being from Paul. This book is therefore a collation of thirteen epistles and those passages from Acts that record the words of Paul *as* the words of Paul. In the nature of the case, words contributed by Silvanus, Timothy, and Sosthenes are also included. Those would be indicated with a footnote if we knew which ones they were.

I did all this rearranging beginning with the King James Version of the English text, and when I had something big enough to work with, I began modernizing and adjusting the language, and working on the transitions. The end result of this is what I trust is a coherent rendering of Paul's thought in a way that reflects both a dynamic equivalence approach to the meaning of the text, and a systematic approach to his theology.

But this also requires explanation. First, by using the phrase *dynamic equivalence*, I do not mean to indicate that this work represents in any way a fresh translation from the Greek. This collation is *not* being presented as a *translation* of the original Greek. This is simply an interpretive rendering of Paul's thought in the form of a "reader's edition." While I did check the Greek occasionally, I was working from older forms of English to contemporary English, and because I was interlarding the book of Romans with pieces of, say, Galatians, *this necessarily meant* that I was giving the contextual flow of Romans seniority, and the contextual flow of the book of Galatians was being largely ignored. If you are reading along and find yourself wondering which specific part of Paul's corpus you're reading, simply check the endnotes. There you'll find the original source for everything in this book.

Second, even though this is not a fresh translation, there is an analogy to translation here nonetheless. When formal equivalence translations are compared to dynamic equivalence translations, an assumption is often made that the difference between them is one of "high" and "low," loftiness of speech versus casualness, when it is actually a distinction of "tight" and "loose." Dynamic equivalence translations often are seen as bringing the language of Scripture *down* to a more breezy or casual level. Thus we wind up with editions of the Bible pitched toward big wave surfers or study Bibles for Old Navy shoppers, and we identify the thing we are doing with the looser approach to translation as a necessary tendency of that approach. But it is quite possible for a dynamic equivalence rendering to go "higher" than the original, or to stay at the same level.

Formal equivalence seeks to stick as closely as possible to the original language, even including such things as word order. In the KJV, for example, if a word not in the original is supplied for the sake of intelligibility, that word is placed in italics so that the reader knows that it was not in the Greek. Dynamic equivalence feels free to adjust the word order for the sake of readability, and is not nearly as tight. And an even looser approach than that is what we find in a paraphrase. I make this point simply to make it clear that this modern rendering is making no attempt at linguistic outreach to lesbians, skateboarders, or millennial chai drinkers.

At places, this rendering remains as formally equivalent as the KJV original was. In other places, it would be better described as dynamic equivalence, and at other places it is paraphrase. That is, it should be described this way as *compared* to the original, and not because it was taken in this way *from* the original. And in other ways and senses, it is best understood as an interpretation and as a commentary. In short, I am not quite sure what this is.

But I do know it is being offered to *readers*, and is not intended for close study of the text. If a particular rendering is evocative and the reader wants to pursue a particular thought, the best thing to do is locate the original passage (identified by means of the endnotes), and to pursue the question with his usual Bible and/or commentaries. In short, the best way to think of this work would be as a commentary or a devotional. In other words, the larger context will not be at all inspired.

So here is my suggestion on how to read this assemblage of Paul's words. Read it straight through, left to right, or browse as you please. Think of it as putting a familiar playlist of songs on shuffle. You know how that usually goes. When you have listened to a playlist for a while, when one song ends, you start to "expect" the next song. You anticipate. You know which one it is, and so you lean into it. You are used to the familiar. When you shuffle the playlist, you might hear the next song with fresh ears. You might be a little surprised. You might think about it.

Of course there is a kind of ignorance that is the result of no familiarity at all. I am entirely ignorant of what it feels like to hike across Nepal. But there is another kind of ignorance, one resulting from excessive familiarity. One time I was driving out to the west side of our small little town——and it is a *small* town——and I was driving on a street I had been on many times before. I had been driving west on that street for decades. And on this occasion, I happened to glance over to the left side of the road and saw a building——an *old* building——which I had never in my life seen before. It was an entire novelty.

By placing everything Paul said around a familiar structure, that of Romans, and by arranging very familiar passages thematically, I believe that an opportunity exists to see some important things that Paul was saying, perhaps for the first time. I am not trying to despise the importance of context. I am trying to arrange things so that the reader stops short, and mutters "wait a minute" to himself. If he reaches for his regular Bible and opens

it up to check the context that God gave it, but somehow
is seeing that context for the first time——even though it
has been there the entire time——then I will consider this
modest venture a success.

Douglas Wilson
On the 500th anniversary of the Reformation

THE COMPLETE

PAUL

A NEW ARRANGEMENT
of the APOSTLE'S WORDS

GRACE AND PEACE

P aul,[1] a prisoner and apostle of Jesus Christ[2] and a servant of God and of[3] Jesus Christ, by the will of God[4] and by the commandment of God our Savior, and the Lord Jesus Christ, according to the faith of God's elect, and the acknowledging of the truth which is according to godliness,[5] which is our hope,[6] according to the promise of life which is in Christ Jesus,[7] called to be an apostle,[8] an apostle of Jesus Christ by the will of God,[9] not of men, nor by man, but by Jesus Christ, and by God the Father, who raised Him from the dead;[10] separated unto the gospel of God——which He had promised beforehand by His prophets in the Holy Scriptures——concerning His Son Jesus Christ our Lord, who was made of the seed of David according to the flesh, and declared to be the Son of God with power, according to the spirit of holiness, by the resurrection from the dead.[11]

This is all in hope of eternal life, which God, who cannot lie, promised before the world began, but which He has in due time manifested His word through preaching, which is committed to me according to the command of God our Savior.[12]

By whom we have received grace and apostleship, for obedience unto the faith among all nations, for His name, to which I was ordained a preacher and an apostle. I speak the truth in Christ, and do not lie. I was made a teacher of the Gentiles in faith and truth,[13] among whom are you also the called of Jesus Christ.[14]

To all who are in Rome, beloved of God, called to be saints;[15] to Timothy, my own dearly beloved[16] son in the faith;[17] to Titus, my own son in our common faith;[18] to the churches of Galatia,[19] to the saints and faithful brothers[20] who are in Ephesus and Colossae, and who are the faithful in Christ Jesus;[21] and to the church of the Thessalonians, which is in God our Father and in the Lord Jesus Christ,[22] and to the church of God which is at Corinth, with all the saints who are in all Achaia: to those who are sanctified in Christ Jesus, called to be saints, with all those who in every place call upon the name of Jesus Christ our Lord, both theirs and ours.[23]

Grace to you, mercy[24] and peace from God our Father, and the Lord Jesus Christ,[25] our Lord,[26] our Savior,[27] the one who gave Himself for our sins, that He might deliver us from this present evil age, according to the will of our God and Father, to whom be glory for ever and ever. Amen.[28]

From Paul, Silvanus, and Timothy our brother, and Sosthenes our brother,[29] and all the brethren which are with me.[30] Timothy our brother and I, servants of Jesus Christ,[31] greet Philemon our dearly beloved, and fellow-laborer, and our beloved Apphia, and Archippus our fellow-soldier, and to the church in your house,[32] as well as all the saints in Christ Jesus which are at Philippi, together with the bishops and deacons.[33] For we have great joy and consolation in your love, because the hearts of the saints are refreshed by you, brother.[34]

DEEP THANKS

First, I thank my God through Jesus Christ for all of you, in that your faith is spoken of throughout the whole world.[35] I thank my God, making mention of you always in my prayers, hearing of your love and faith, which you have toward the Lord Jesus, and toward all saints, that the fellowship of your faith may be efficacious by the acknowledgment of every good thing which you have in Christ Jesus.[36]

I thank my God for every memory of you, always in every prayer for you making my requests with joy, for your fellowship in the gospel from the first day until now. I do this confident of this very thing, that He who has begun a good work in you will complete it at the day of Jesus Christ. It is fitting for me to think this of you all, because I have you in my heart——because both in my bonds, and in the defense and confirmation of the gospel, you all are partakers of my grace. For God is my witness, how greatly I long for you all in the compassion of Jesus Christ. And this I pray, that your love may abound even more and more in knowledge and in all discernment; so that you may approve the things that are excellent, that you may be sincere and without blame until the day of Christ, and that you may be filled with the fruits of righteousness, which are by Jesus Christ to the glory and praise of God.[37]

We give thanks to God, the Father of our Lord Jesus Christ, praying always for you, ever since we heard of your faith in Christ Jesus, and of the love which you have for all the saints. This comes from the hope which is laid up for you in heaven, which you heard about in the word of the truth of the gospel, which has come to you, as it has to all the world, bringing forth fruit, as it has also in you, since the day you first heard of it, and knew the grace of God in truth. You learned this from Epaphras, our dear fellow servant, who is for you a faithful minister of Christ, and who also declared to us your love in the Spirit.[38]

We are bound always to thank God for you, brothers, as it is fitting, because your faith grows greatly, and the love of each one of you all toward each other abounds. So then we ourselves glory in you in the churches of God for your patience and faith in all your persecutions and tribulations that you endure, which is a manifest token of the righteous judgment of God, that you might be counted worthy of the kingdom of God, for which reason you now suffer, seeing that it is a righteous thing for God to recompense tribulation to those who trouble you.[39]

But we are bound to give thanks to God for you always, as brothers beloved of the Lord, because God has from the beginning chosen you for salvation through the sanctification of the Spirit and belief in the truth. This is how He called you by our gospel, to obtain the glory of our Lord Jesus Christ. Therefore, brothers, stand fast, and hold fast the traditions which you have been taught, either by word or our epistle. Now our Lord Jesus Christ Himself, and God, even our Father, who has loved us, and has given us everlasting consolation and good hope through grace, comfort your hearts, and establish you in every good word and work.[40]

On your behalf, I thank my God always for the grace of God which is given to you by Jesus Christ, that in everything you be enriched by Him, in all speech and in all knowledge, just as the testimony of Christ was confirmed in you, so that you lag behind in no gift, as you wait for the coming of our Lord Jesus Christ. He is the one who will also confirm you to the end, so that you may be blameless in the day of our Lord Jesus Christ. God is faithful, by whom you were called into the fellowship of His Son Jesus Christ our Lord.[41]

Blessed be God, the Father of our Lord Jesus Christ, the Father of mercies, and the God of all comfort. He comforts us in all our afflictions in order that we might be able to comfort those who are in any trouble, using the comfort by which we ourselves were comforted by God. For just as the sufferings of Christ abound in us, so also our consolation abounds by Christ. And if we are afflicted, it is for your consolation and salvation, which is effectual in your endurance of the same sufferings which we also suffer. And if we are comforted, it is for your consolation and salvation. And our hope for you is steadfast, knowing that as you are partakers of the sufferings, in the same way you will partake of the consolation.[42]

For this same reason we also, since the day we first heard it, have not ceased to pray for you, desiring that you would be filled with the knowledge of His will in all wisdom and spiritual understanding. We desire that you might walk worthy of the Lord, pleasing Him fully. We want you fruitful in every good work, increasing in the knowledge of God, strengthened with all might——according to His glorious power, with the result of all patience and endurance with joy. We desire that you give thanks to the Father, who has made us ready to be partakers of the inheritance of the saints in light, who has delivered us from the power of darkness, and has translated us into the kingdom of His dear Son, in whom we have redemption through His blood, that is to say, the forgiveness of sins. He is the image of the invisible God, the firstborn of all creation.[43]

We give thanks to God for all of you at all times, making mention of you in our prayers. Without ceasing, we remember your work of faith, your labor of love, and patience of hope in our Lord Jesus Christ, in the sight of God and our Father. We do this, beloved brothers, knowing your election of God. For our gospel came to you, not only in word, but also in power, and in the Holy Ghost, and in much assurance. For you know what kind of men we were among you for your sake. And so you became followers of us, and also of the Lord, having received the word in much affliction, with joy in the Holy Spirit. This happened such that you were examples to all who believed in Macedonia and Achaia. For from you the Word of the

Lord sounded forth, not only in Macedonia and Achaia, but also in every place your God-ward faith spread everywhere——so that we do not need to say anything. For these reports themselves demonstrate what manner of entrance we had to you, and how you turned to God from idols, in order to serve the living and true God, and to wait for His Son from heaven, whom He raised from the dead, even Jesus——who delivered us from the wrath to come.[44]

AFFLICTION AND PEACE

For, brothers, we would not want you to be ignorant of the trouble which came to us in Asia, such that we were burdened beyond measure, far above our strength, so that we despaired even of our lives. But we had the sentence of death in ourselves so that we should not trust in ourselves, but rather in God who raises the dead. He delivered us from that deadly threat, and does deliver us, so that we trust He will continue to deliver us. You also help in this by praying for us, so that many will offer thanks for the blessing given to us through the prayers of many people, such that for the gift bestowed upon us by the means of many people thanks may be given by many on our behalf.[45]

Though it is not helpful for me to boast, I will come to visions and revelations of the Lord. I knew a man in Christ over fourteen years ago——whether in the body, I cannot tell; or out of the body, I cannot tell: God knows——this man was caught up to the third heaven. And I knew such a man——whether in the body, or out of the body, I cannot tell: God knows——who was caught up into paradise, and heard ineffable words, which are not lawful for a man to say. Of this man I will boast, but in myself I will not boast, unless it is in my infirmities. For though I might desire to boast, I will not be a fool. I will only speak the truth, but for now I forbear——lest any man thinks of me above what he sees me to be, or above what he hears of me.

And in case I should be unduly exalted through the greatness of the revelations, I was given in the flesh, a messenger of Satan, to buffet me, lest I be exalted above due measure. Because of this I pleaded with the Lord three times, that it might be taken from me. But He said to me, "My grace is sufficient for you——for my strength is made perfect in weakness." Therefore I will most gladly glory in my infirmities, so that the power of Christ may rest upon me. This is why I take pleasure in infirmities, insults, hardships, afflictions, and disasters for Christ's sake. For when I am weak, then I am strong. I am boasting like a fool, but you have made me. I ought rather to have been commended by you, for in nothing do I lag behind the most eminent apostles, even though I am nothing. For indeed, the signs of an apostle were done among you with all endurance, with signs, and wonders, and great deeds. In what way were you inferior to the other churches, except that I was in no way burdensome to you? Forgive me this great wrong.[46]

So then, as workers together with Him, we plead with you also that you do not receive the grace of God in vain. For He has said, "I have heard you in an accepted time, and in the day of salvation I have nourished you——behold, now is the accepted time; behold, now is the day of salvation." We give no offense in anything in order that the ministry will not be faulted, but rather in all things showing ourselves approved as ministers of God——in great endurance, in afflictions, in trials, in disasters, in beatings, in imprisonments, in riots, in labors, in sleepless nights, in fasts; by purity, by knowledge, by patience, by kindness, by the Holy Spirit, by unfeigned love, by the word of truth, by the power of God; with the armory of righteousness for the right hand and for the left; through honor and dishonor, through slander and good report. We are thought to be frauds, and yet are true; as nobodies, and yet famous; as dying, and yet, behold, we live; as punished, and yet still alive; as sorrowful, yet always rejoicing; as poor, yet making many others rich; as having nothing, and yet possessing everything.[47]

In addition, when I came to Troas to preach the gospel of Christ, and finding a door opened to me by the Lord, I still had no rest in my spirit because I did not find Titus my brother there. So taking my leave of them, I went from there into Macedonia. Now thanks be to God, who always causes us to triumph in Christ, and makes manifest the fragrance of His knowledge in every place through us. For we are before God a sweet aroma of Christ, in those who are saved, and with those who perish. To the one we are the aroma of death unto death; and to the other the aroma of life unto life. And who is sufficient for these things? For we are not as many others, who corrupt the word of God——we speak in Christ from all sincerity, as of God, and in the sight of God.[48]

HONEST MINISTRY

Therefore seeing that we have this ministry, as we have received mercy, we do not faint. We have renounced hidden and dishonest things, not walking in craftiness, nor handling the word of God deceitfully, but rather through manifestation of the truth we commend ourselves to every man's conscience in the sight of God. If our gospel is hidden, it is hidden to those who are lost——those in whom the god of this world has blinded their unbelieving minds, lest the light of the glorious gospel of Christ——who is the image of God—— should shine on them. For we do not preach ourselves, but rather Christ Jesus as Lord, and ourselves as your slaves for Jesus' sake. For God, who commanded the light to shine out of darkness, has shined in our hearts, to give the light of the knowledge of the glory of God in the face of Jesus Christ.[49]

For our rejoicing is in this——the testimony of our conscience——that in simplicity and godly sincerity, not with carnal wisdom, but by the grace of God, we have conducted our lives in the world, and more abundantly toward you all. For we write nothing else to you than what you read and understand, and that I trust you shall understand even to the end——just as you have understood us partially, that on the day of the Lord Jesus, you will boast in us just as we boast in you. And in this assurance, I had thought to come to first, that you might have a second blessing. I wanted to visit you on the way to Macedonia, and to come again to you out of Macedonia, and to be helped by you on my way to Judea. When I thought to do this, was I being flighty? The things that I intend, do I intend them according to the flesh, so that from me there should be *yes, yes*, and *no, no* at the same time?[50]

Now I call God against my soul——it was to spare you that I did not come to Corinth. Not for that we have dominion over your faith, but we work with you for your joy, for it is by faith you stand.[51]

For I decided in my own mind that I would not come again to you in another painful visit. For if I bring you sorrow, who is there to make me glad except the one I made sorrowful? And so I wrote to you as I did so that, when I come, I would not have sorrow in those that should bring me joy. I had this confidence in all of you, that my joy would be yours. I wrote to you out of much affliction and anguish of heart, with many tears, not that you would be grieved, but that you might know the abundant love which I have toward you.

But if anyone has caused grief, it was not to me but——not to be too severe——to a certain extent to all of you. This man's discipline is sufficient, which was imposed by the many, meaning that to the contrary you should forgive him now, and comfort him, lest he be swallowed up with excessive sorrow. Therefore I plead with you to confirm your love toward him. This is why I wrote to you, so that I might test you, seeing if you would be obedient in all things. If you forgive anything, I forgive it also. And if I forgive anything, for your sakes I forgive the one I forgive——in the person of Christ. I do this lest Satan get an advantage over us, for we are not ignorant of his devices.[52]

Consider——this is the third time I am prepared to come to you. I will not be a burden to you, for I do not seek what is yours, but rather *you*. Children ought not to save up for their parents, but instead the parents for the children. And I am very glad to spend and be spent for you, even if the more abundantly I love you, the less I am loved. Even so, I did not burden you——but, crafty as I am, I must have trapped you with guile. But did I make a profit from you by any of those I sent unto you? I chose Titus, and I sent a brother with him. Did Titus make a profit off you? Did we not walk in the same spirit? Did we not walk in the same steps?

Again, do you think we are making excuses to you? We speak before God in Christ, but dearly beloved, we do all things for your edification. For I fear that when I come, I will not find you in the condition I desire, and that I will be found undesirable by you as well. I am speaking of debates, tangles of envy, anger, conflicts, backbiting, whisperings, swellings, and controversy. And I fear that, when I come to you again, my God will humble me among you, and that I shall have to mourn many who have sinned already, and have not repented of the uncleanness and fornication and lasciviousness of which they are guilty.[53]

This is the third time I am coming to you. In the mouth of two or three witnesses every word needs to be established. I told you before, and tell you this again beforehand, as though I were already present, just like the second time. And being absent currently I write to those who have sinned earlier, and to any others that, if I come again, I will not go easy. I do this since you seek proof that Christ speaks through me, which toward you is not weak, but rather is mighty in your midst. For though He was crucified in weakness, yet He lives by the power of God. For we also are weak in Him, but we shall live with Him by the power of God toward you. Examine yourselves then, to see if you are really in the faith; test your own selves. Don't you know your own selves, how Jesus Christ is in you——unless you are found reprobates? But I trust you will know that *we* are not reprobates.

RECIPROCAL PRAYERS

Now I pray to God that you do no evil, not that *we* would seem approved, but so that you might do that which is honest——even if we come off as reprobates. For we can do nothing against the truth, but only for the truth. For we are glad when we are weak and you strong——this is what we wish for, even your maturity. Therefore I write this way even though absent——if I were present I would be sharp with you, according to the authority which the Lord gave me for edification, and not for destruction.[54]

I thank God, whom I serve with a pure conscience, down from my forefathers, that without ceasing I have remembered you in my prayers both night and day. I have greatly desired to see you, mindful of your tears, that I may be filled with joy when I call to mind the sincere faith that is in you——the same faith which first dwelt in your grandmother Lois, and your mother Eunice, and which I am persuaded is in you also. This is why I put you in remembrance to stir up the gift of God which is in you through the laying on of my hands. For God has not given us the spirit of timidity, but rather of power, and of love, and of a sound mind. So do not be ashamed of the testimony of our Lord, or of me His prisoner. Rather be a partaker of the afflictions of the gospel according to the power of God, who has saved us and called us with a holy calling, not according to our works, but according to His own purpose and grace, which was given us in Christ Jesus before the world began. This grace is now made manifest by the appearing of our Savior Jesus Christ, who has abolished death, and has brought life and immortality to light through the gospel.[55]

Finally, brothers, pray for us. Pray that the word of the Lord may have a free run, and be glorified, even as happened among you. And pray that we may be delivered from unreasonable and wicked men——for not all men have faith. But the Lord is faithful, who will establish you and keep you from evil. And we have confidence in the Lord concerning you, that you are both doing and will continue to do the things which we command you. And may the Lord direct your hearts into the love of God, and into a patient waiting for Christ.[56]

This is why I also, after I heard of your faith in the Lord Jesus, and your love for all the saints, never stopped giving thanks for you, making mention of you in my prayers. I asked that the God of our Lord Jesus Christ, the Father of glory, might give to you the spirit of wisdom and revelation in the knowledge of Him, with the eyes of your understanding being enlightened, that you might know what is the hope of His calling, and what are the riches of the glory of His inheritance in the saints, along with the exceeding greatness of His power toward us who believe, according to the working of His mighty power.

This power He wrought in Christ, when He raised Him from the dead and set Him at His own right hand in the heavenly places, far above all principality, and power, and might, and dominion, and every name that is named, not only in this age, but also in the one which is to come. And He has put all things under His feet, and gave Him to be the head over all things for the church, which is His body, the fullness of Him that fills all in all.[57]

PERSONAL HISTORY

But I can assure you, brothers, the gospel which was preached by me is not according to man. For I neither received it from man, nor was taught it, but rather from a revelation of Jesus Christ. For you have heard of my former way of life in the religion of Judaism, and how I persecuted the church of God beyond measure, and wasted it. I excelled in my pursuit of Judaism, surpassing many of my peers among my own people, being as I was far more zealous than they in the traditions of my fathers. But then it pleased God, who had separated me from my mother's womb, and had called me by His grace, to reveal His Son in me, so that I might preach Him among the Gentiles. Immediately——I did not confer with flesh and blood, and did not go up to Jerusalem to speak to those who were apostles before me——I went into Arabia, and returned afterward again to Damascus. After three years I went up to Jerusalem to see Peter, and stayed with him for fifteen days. But I did not see any of the other apostles except for James, the Lord's brother. Now in the sight of God, these things I write to you are no lies. Afterward I came to the regions of Syria and Cilicia. I was unknown by sight to the churches of Judaea which were in Christ. They only heard that the one who used to persecute is now preaching the faith he once sought to destroy. And they glorified God because of me.

But as God Himself is true, our word to you was not *yes* and *no*. For the Son of God, Jesus Christ, who was preached among you by us——by me and Silas and Timothy——was not yes and no, but in Him was only *yes*. For all the promises of God in Him are *yes*, and in Him *amen*, to the glory of God by us. Now He who establishes us together with you in Christ, and has anointed us, is God, who has also sealed us, and given us the earnest payment of the Spirit in our hearts.[58]

In addition, brothers, I declare to you the gospel which I preached to you earlier, which you have received, and in which you stand. By this you are saved if you keep in memory what I preached unto you——unless you believed in vain. For I delivered to you first of all what I also received, which is that Christ died for our sins according to the Scriptures, and that He was buried, and that He rose again on the third day according to the Scriptures. He was seen by Cephas, and then by the twelve. After that, He was seen by over five hundred brothers at once, of whom the majority remain down to the present, although some have fallen asleep. After that, He was seen by James, and by all the apostles. And last of all, He was seen by me also, as someone born at the wrong time. For I am the least of the apostles, and am not fit to be called an apostle, because I persecuted the church of God. But by the grace of God I am what I am, and His grace bestowed on me was not given in vain——I have labored more abundantly than all of them, but it was not I, but rather the grace of God which was with me. Therefore whether it was I or they, so we preach, and so you believed.[59]

I am a man who is a Jew from Tarsus, a city in Cilicia, a citizen of no contemptible city. I would plead with you to allow me to speak to the people.

King Agrippa, I consider myself fortunate that I may answer for myself this day before you, concerning all the things I am accused of by the Jews. This is especially so because I know you to be expert in all the customs and questions which are among the Jews. I therefore ask you to hear me patiently. So men, brothers, and fathers, hear now my defense which I would make now to you.

I truly am a man who is a Jew, born in Tarsus, a city in Cilicia, yet brought up here in this city at the feet of Gamaliel, taught according to the correct manner of the law of our fathers, and was zealous for God, as all of you are this day. All the Jews know my manner of life from my youth, which from the beginning was in Jerusalem and among my own people. Those who knew me then can testify that I lived according to the strictest sect of our religion, living as Pharisee. And I persecuted followers of this way to the death, binding and delivering both men and women into prison. I myself was completely convinced that I ought to do many things against the name of Jesus of Nazareth. This is what I did in Jerusalem——many of the saints I shut up in prison, having received authorization from the chief priests. And when they were put to death, my vote was against them. And I punished them frequently in every synagogue, and attempted to compel them to blaspheme. Exceedingly enraged against them, I persecuted them even into foreign cities. The high priest could bear me witness, and the entire council of elders, from whom I received letters to the brothers. With those on one such occasion I went to Damascus, my authority and commission from the chief priests in hand, to bring those that I bound there to Jerusalem to be punished.

And it came about that as I made my journey, and came near to Damascus around noon, suddenly a great light from heaven shone round about me. It was beyond the brightness of the sun, shining all around me and those who traveled with me. When we had all fallen to the earth, I heard a voice in the Hebrew language saying to me, "Saul, Saul, why do you persecute me? It is hard for you to kick against the goads." And I answered, "Who are you, Lord?" And He said to me, "I am Jesus of Nazareth, whom you are persecuting. But rise, stand up on your feet. For I have appeared to you for this reason, in order to make you a minister and a witness——of both the things you have seen, and the things I will reveal to you. I will deliver you from the people, and from the Gentiles, unto whom I am now sending you. I send you to open their eyes, to turn them from darkness to light, and from the power of Satan to God, in order that they might receive forgiveness of sins, and an inheritance among those who are sanctified by faith in me."

And those who were with me indeed saw the light, and were afraid, but they could not hear the voice of the one who spoke to me. And I said, "What shall I do, Lord?" And the Lord said to me, "Arise, and go into Damascus, and there you will be told all the things which are appointed to you to do."

Because I could not see because of the glory of that light, I was led by the hand by those who were with me, and I came into Damascus. And one Ananias, a devout man according to the law, a man with a good report from all the Jews who dwelt there, came to me, and stood over me, and said to me, "Brother Saul, receive your sight." And that same hour I looked up at him. And he said, "The God of our fathers has chosen you, that you should know His will, and see that Just One, and should hear the voice of His mouth. For you will be His witness to all men of what you have seen and heard. And now, why do you delay? Arise, and be baptized, and wash away your sins, calling on the name of the Lord.

Therefore, O King Agrippa, I was not disobedient to the heavenly vision. I first showed those in Damascus, then at Jerusalem, and then throughout all the territory of Judaea, and then out to the Gentiles, that they should repent and turn to God, and do works that show real repentance. For these reasons the Jews caught me in the Temple, and attempted to kill me. But having obtained help from God, I continue down to this day, witnessing both to small and great, saying nothing other than what the prophets and Moses said would come——that Christ would suffer, and that He would be the first man to rise from the dead, and who would shed light on the people, and on the Gentiles.

And it happened that——when I came again to Jerusalem——even while I was praying in the temple, I fell into a trance. And I saw Him saying to me, "Make haste, and get yourself out of Jerusalem quickly. For they will not receive your testimony concerning me." And I said, "Lord, they know that I imprisoned and beat all those who believed in you——in every synagogue. And when the blood of your martyr Stephen was shed, I also was standing by, consenting to his death, and I guarded the clothing of those who killed him." And He said to me, "Depart, for I will send you far from here to the Gentiles.

And now it is that I stand and am judged for the hope of the promise made by God to our fathers. This is the promise which our twelve tribes, eagerly serving God day and night, hope to obtain. For the sake of this hope, King Agrippa, I am accused by the Jews. Why should it be thought an incredible thing by you that God should raise the dead?

I am not mad, most noble Festus, and I speak the words of truth and sobriety. For the king knows about these things, and I may speak freely before him. For I am persuaded that none of these things are hidden away from him——this thing was not accomplished in a corner. King Agrippa, do you believe the prophets? I know that you believe.[60]

But you have known my doctrine fully, along with my manner of life, purpose, faith, patience, love, steadfastness, together with the persecutions and afflictions which came upon me at Antioch, Iconium, and Lystra. What persecutions I endured!——but the Lord delivered me out of them all. Yes——all who desire to live a godly life in Christ Jesus will endure persecution. But evil men and seducers shall grow worse and worse, both deceiving and being deceived.[61]

Now I also thank Christ Jesus our Lord, who has enabled me by putting me into ministry, counting me faithful. He did this even though I was a blasphemer, a persecutor, and an insolent man. But I obtained mercy because I acted in ignorant unbelief. And the grace of our Lord was overflowing toward me with the faith and love that is in Christ Jesus. This is a faithful saying, and worthy of all acceptance, that Christ Jesus came into the world in order to save sinners, with me as the foremost. However for this reason I obtained mercy, that with me foremost, Jesus Christ might display His utter patience, as a template for those who would later believe in Him to everlasting life.[62]

Now fourteen years afterwards, I went up again to Jerusalem with Barnabas, and took Titus with me also. I went there as a result of a revelation, and communicated to them the gospel which I preach among the Gentiles.

I did this privately for those who had some reputation, lest failure to do so would mean I was running, or had run, in vain. Now Titus was with me, a Greek, and he was not compelled to be circumcised. The issue only arose because false brothers had unknowingly been brought in, who were there secretly to spy out the liberty which we have in Christ Jesus——in order to bring us into slavery. We did not give way to these men by submission, no, not even for an hour, so that the truth of the gospel might continue with you.

But for those who seemed to be someone significant—— whatever they were made no difference to me; God accepts no personages——those who seemed significant in that conference added nothing to me. To the contrary, when they saw that the gospel of the uncircumcision was committed to me, as the gospel of the circumcision had been to Peter, they extended the hand of fellowship. For He who worked effectually in Peter's apostleship to the circumcision, that same one was mighty in me toward the Gentiles. So when James, Cephas, and John, who seemed to be pillars, grasped the grace that had been given to me, they extended to me and to Barnabas the right hand of fellowship, such that we should go to the Gentiles, and they to the circumcision. They only asked that we would continue to remember the poor, the very thing we had come to do and were eager to do.

But when Peter came to Antioch, I withstood him to his face, because he was at fault. For before certain men came from James, he would eat with the Gentiles, but after they arrived, he withdrew and separated himself——fearing those who were of the circumcision faction. And there were other Jews who dissembled in the same way with him, insofar as that even Barnabas was carried off with their hypocrisy. So when I saw that they were not walking uprightly in line with the truth of the gospel, I said to Peter in front of them all, "If you, being a Jew, live like a Gentile, and not the way the Jews do, why do you compel the Gentiles to live like the Jews?" We who are Jews by nature, and not sinners of the Gentiles, are still justified by faith.[63]

ENTRUSTED WITH
THE GOSPEL

In the cause of this faith I am appointed a preacher, and an apostle, and a teacher of the Gentiles. This is why I suffer what I do——nevertheless I am not ashamed, for I know whom I have believed, and am persuaded that He is able to keep that which I have committed to Him against that day.[64]

For you yourselves know, brothers, that our first entry with you was not in vain. Even after we had suffered earlier, and were shamefully treated at Philippi, as you know, we were still bold in our God to speak to you the gospel of God despite much opposition. For our exhortation was not from deceit, or uncleanness, or in guile.

But since we were allowed by God to be entrusted with the gospel, in that way we speak——not as trying to please men, but rather God, who tests our hearts. For at no time did we use flattering words, as you well know, or as a covering for covetousness——God is witness. Neither did we seek glory from men, whether from you or others, when we could have been a burden to you as apostles of Christ. But rather we were gentle with you, as a nursing mother cherishing her children.

So having affectionate desire for you, we were willing to have our own souls given to you, and not the gospel

of God only——because you were dear to us. For you remember, brothers, our labor and travail. We worked night
and day because we would not be charged to any of you,
and so we preached to you the gospel of God. You are witnesses, and God is also a witness, how holy and just and
blameless our behavior was among you who believed. You
know how we exhorted and comforted and charged every
one of you——the way a father does his children——that
you would walk worthy of God, who has called you into
His kingdom and glory. For this reason we also thank God
without ceasing because, when you received the word of
God which you heard from us, you received it not as the
word of men, but as it is in truth, the word of God, which
effectually works also in you who believe.[65]

For God is my witness——whom I serve in my spirit
in the gospel of his Son——that without ceasing I always
make mention of you in my prayers. My request is that it
be the will of God if by any means I finally might have a
prosperous journey to come to you. For I long to see you,
in order that I might impart to you some spiritual gift, so
that you might be established. What I mean is that I might
be comforted together with you by our mutual faith, both
yours and mine.

Now I would not leave you in ignorance, brothers,
that I *often* intended to come to you, but up to this point
was prevented. I wanted to come so that I might have
some fruit among you also, even as I do among other Gentiles. I am a debtor both to Greeks, and to the

barbarians, both to the wise and to the unwise. So as much as lies with me, I am ready to preach the gospel to you who are in Rome also.[66]

I am amazed that you are so quickly removed from the one who called you into the grace of Christ over to another gospel——which is actually not another gospel, but there are some who would trouble you, wanting to pervert the gospel of Christ. But even if we (or an angel from heaven) preach any other gospel to you than the one which we preached to you at first, let him be damned. As we said before, and I now say again, if any man preach any other gospel to you than what you have already received, then let him be *damned*. Now do I now persuade men or God? Or do I seek to please men? If the point were to please men, I would not be a slave of Christ.[67]

For I am not ashamed of the gospel of Christ——it is the power of God to salvation for every one that believes, to the Jew first, and then to the Greek. For in it the righteousness of God is revealed from faith to faith, as it is written, "The just shall live by faith." For the wrath of God is revealed from heaven against all the ungodliness and unrighteousness of men, who hold down the truth in their unrighteousness.

THE CONDITION OF MAN

That which may be known of God is manifest within them, for God has shown it to them. For His invisible traits have been clearly seen from the creation of the world, being understood through the things that are made, meaning His eternal power and Godhead, so that they are without excuse. This is because, although they knew God, they refused to glorify Him as God, and neither were they thankful. Rather, they became vain in their imaginations, and their foolish hearts were darkened. Professing themselves to be wise, they became fools, and exchanged the glory of the incorruptible God for an image made like corruptible man, or to birds, or four-footed beasts, or creeping things. As a consequence, God gave them up to uncleanness through the lusts of their own hearts, such that they would dishonor their own bodies among themselves, those who had changed the truth of God into a lie, and who had worshipped and served the creature more than the Creator, who is blessed for ever. Amen.

For this reason God gave them over to vile affections. Even their women changed the natural use into that which is against nature, as did likewise the men, abandoning the natural use of the woman, burning in their lust one toward another. Men did with men that which is shameless, and received in themselves the recompense of their error which was fitting. And just as they did not want to retain God in their knowledge, God gave them over to a reprobate mind, to do those things which are not right——being filled with all unrighteousness, fornication, evil, covetousness, malice. They are filled with envy, murder, strife, deceit, malevolence. They are gossips, backbiters, haters of God, insolent, arrogant, boastful, inventors of evil, disobedient to parents. They are without understanding, feckless, without normal affection, implacable, ruthless. They know the judgment of God concerning these things, that those who commit them are worthy of death, but they not only do them, but take pleasure in the fact that others do them.[68]

So this is what I therefore say, testifying to it in the Lord, that from this point you do not walk as other Gentiles walk, in the vanity of their mind, with their understanding darkened, being alienated from the life of God on account of the ignorance that is in them because of the blindness of their heart——who being callused have given themselves over to sensuality, greedy for every form of impurity. But you have not learned Christ in this way, on the assumption that you heard Him, and were taught by Him, as the truth is in Jesus, to put off the old man, which is consistent with your former way of life, and which is corrupted by lying desires, and that you be renewed in the spirit of your mind, and that you put on the new man, which was created in the likeness of God in righteousness and true holiness. Therefore put away lying, and let every man speak truth to his neighbor, for we are members one of another. Be angry, but do not sin in it. Do not let the sun go down on your anger, refusing to give way to the devil. Let the thief steal no longer, but rather let him labor, working with his hands at an honest job, that he may have substance of his own to give to those who need it. Let no corrupt discourse come out of your mouth, but only that which contributes to edification, that it may minister grace to those who hear it. And do not grieve the Holy Spirit of God, by whom you were sealed for the day of redemption. Let all bitterness, and wrath, and anger, and clamor, and slander be put away from you, along with all malice. And be *kind* to one another, tenderhearted, forgiving one another, in just the way that God forgave you for the sake of Christ.[69]

And you who were at one time alienated and enemies in your minds through wicked acts, yet He has now reconciled through the body of His flesh through death, in order to present you holy and blameless, irreproachable in His sight; that is, if you continue in the faith grounded and settled, and are not moved away from the hope of the gospel, which you have heard, and which has been preached to every creature that is under heaven, and of which, I, Paul, have been made a minister. And I now rejoice in my sufferings for you, and fill up in my flesh that which is lacking in the afflictions of Christ for His body's sake, which is the church, of which I was made a minister, according to the stewardship of God which was given to me for you, in order to fulfil the word of God, that is, the mystery which has been hidden for ages and generations, but is now made manifest to His saints——to whom God would make known the riches of the glory of this mystery among the Gentiles, which is Christ in you, the hope of glory, the one we preach, warning every man, and teaching every man in all wisdom, in order to present every man perfect in Christ Jesus. And to this end I labor, striving according to His working, which works in me mightily.[70]

CHRIST,
THE WISDOM OF GOD

For by Him all things were created, whether in heaven, or on earth, visible and invisible, whether thrones, dominions, principalities, or powers. All things were created by Him, and for Him. And He is before all things, and by Him all things consist. He is the head of the body, the church, and He is the ultimate, the firstborn from the dead——that in all things He might have the preeminence. For it pleased the Father that all fullness should dwell in Him, and having made peace through the blood of His cross, by Him to reconcile all things to Himself——by Him, I tell you, whether they are things in earth or things in heaven.[71]

And brothers, when I came to you, it was not in excellence of speech or in wisdom, declaring to you the testimony of God. For I decided not to know anything among you except for Jesus Christ and Him crucified. I was with you in weakness, and in fear, and in great trembling. And my speech and my preaching was not with the enticing words of man's wisdom, but rather in demonstration of the Spirit and of power——that your faith might not stand in the wisdom of men, but in the power of God.

Nonetheless we speak wisdom among those who are mature——but not the wisdom of this world, nor of the princes of this world, who all come to nothing. But we speak the wisdom of God in a mystery, even the hidden wisdom, which God ordained before the world for our glory. None of the princes of this world knew of it, for if they had known of it, they would not have crucified the Lord of glory. But as it is written, "Eye has not seen, nor ear heard, and neither has it entered the heart of man, the things which God has prepared for those who love Him." But God has revealed them to us by His Spirit——because the Spirit searches all things, yes, even the deep things of God. For what man knows "the things" of a man, except the spirit of man which is within him? In the same way, the things of God are known by no man, but only by the Spirit of God. Now we have not received the spirit of the world, but rather the spirit which is of God——in order that we might know the things that are freely given to us by God. These are the things which we also speak, not in the words that man's wisdom would teach, but rather which the Holy Ghost teaches, comparing spiritual things with spiritual. But the natural man does not receive the things of the Spirit of God; they are foolishness to him and he cannot know them because they are spiritually dis-cerned. But the one who is spiritual judges all things, yet he himself is judged by no man. For who has known the mind of the Lord, that he might instruct Him? But we have the mind of Christ.[72]

Do you look on the outward appearance of things? If any man trust in himself that he is Christ's, let him think this in himself also, that, just as he is Christ's, even so are we Christ's. For though I might boast in our authority——which the Lord has given us for edification, and not for your destruction——I would not be ashamed. I am not trying to terrify you by letter. For His letters, they say, are weighty and powerful, but His bodily presence is weak, and His speech is contemptible. Let such a person think this, that, just as we are in word by letter when we are absent, so also we will be in deed when we are present.

For we dare not include ourselves in the number, or compare ourselves with those who commend themselves——for those who measure themselves by themselves, and compare themselves to themselves, are not wise. But we will not boast of things without a true measure, but rather according to the measure of the rule which God has distributed to us, a measure that also includes you. For we do not stretch ourselves beyond our measure, as though we had not reached to you, for we have come as far as to you in preaching the gospel of Christ. We do not boast of things beyond our measure, that is, of other men's work, but in the hope, when your faith is increased, that we shall be abundantly enlarged by you according to our rule. I mean to preach the gospel in the regions beyond you, and not to boast in another man's work or territory. But he that glories, let him glory in the Lord. For it is not the one who commends himself who is approved, but rather he whom the Lord commends.[73]

THE UNKNOWN GOD

You men of Athens, I perceive that in everything you are quite religious. For as I was walking around, and beheld your sacred things, I found an altar with this inscription——*to the unknown God.* Now whom you worship in ignorance, I declare to you. The God who made the world and all things it contains, seeing that He is Lord of heaven and earth, does not dwell in temples made with hands. Neither is He worshipped with men's hands, as though He needed anything, seeing as He gives life to all, and breath, and everything else. And He has made all nations of men from one blood, in order to dwell on the face of the whole earth, and He has determined the times appointed for them beforehand, along with the boundaries of their habitation. He did this so that they might seek the Lord, if perhaps they might grope after Him, and find Him——even though He is not far from any one of us. For in Him we live, and move, and have our being. And as certain of your own poets have said, "For we are also His offspring." Inasmuch then as we are the offspring of God, we ought not to think that the Godhead is like gold, or silver, or stone, graven by man's artistry and design. Now God winked at these times of ignorance, but He now commands all men everywhere to repent. This is because He has appointed a day in which

He will judge the world in righteousness by that man whom He has ordained, of which He has given assurance to all men by raising Him from the dead.[74]

Men, why do you do these things? We also are men of a similar nature to you, and preach to you that you should turn from these vanities to the living God, who made heaven, and earth, and the sea, and everything in them. He was the one who in times past allowed all nations to walk in their own ways. Nevertheless He did not leave Himself without a witness——in that He did good, and gave us rain from heaven, and fruitful seasons, filling our hearts with food and gladness.[75]

THE CONDITION
OF THE JEWS

Y ou are therefore inexcusable, O man, whenever you judge, for when you judge another, you condemn yourself—you who are judging do the same things. Nevertheless, we are certain that the judgment of God is according to truth against those who commit such things. So do you think, O man, you who judge those who do such things, and do them yourself, that you will escape the judgment of God? Do you despise the riches of His goodness and forbearance and patience, not understanding that the goodness of God is supposed to lead you to repentance? Rather your hardness and impenitence of heart treasures up for yourself wrath for the day of wrath, and the revelation of the righteous judgment of God, who will render to every man in accordance with his deeds.

He will give eternal life to those who by patient continuance in doing good seek for glory and honor and immortality, but to those who are contentious and do not obey the truth, but rather obey unrighteousness, indignation and wrath, He will give tribulation and anguish, for every soul of man that does evil, for the Jew first, and also for the Gentile. But He will give glory, honor, and peace to every man who works what is good, to the Jew first, and also to the Gentile——for there is no respect of persons with God. For as many as have sinned apart from the law shall also perish apart from the law, and as many as have sinned under the law shall be judged by the law. For it is not the hearers of the law who are just before God, but rather the doers of the law who shall be justified. For when the Gentiles, who do not have the law, by nature do the things contained in the law, these, having not the law, are a law unto themselves. They show the work of the law written on their hearts, their conscience bearing witness, and their thoughts at the same time either accusing or excusing one another. This will happen on the day when God shall judge the secrets of men by Jesus Christ according to my gospel.

Behold, you are called a Jew, and rest in the law, and make your boast in God. And you know His will, and approve the more excellent things, being instructed as you are out of the law. You are confident that you yourself are a guide to the blind, a light for those who are in darkness, an instructor of the foolish, and a teacher of babes——having the form of knowledge and of the truth in the law. You therefore who teach others, do you not teach yourself? You who preach that a man should not steal, do you steal? You who say a man should not commit adultery, do you commit adultery? You who abhor idols, are you guilty of sacrilege? You who make your boast in the law, do you dishonor God through breaking the law? For the name of God is blasphemed among the Gentiles because of you, as it is written.

Now circumcision is true profit, if you keep the law, but you are a breaker of the law, your circumcision amounts to uncircumcision. Therefore if the uncircumcised keep the righteousness of the law, will not his uncircumcision be reckoned as circumcision? And shall not natural uncircumcision, if it fulfil the law, judge you, who transgress the law both by the letter and by circumcision? For that man is not a Jew who is one outwardly, and neither is that circumcision which is merely outward in the flesh. But he is a true Jew who is one inwardly, and whose circumcision is of the heart, in the spirit, and not by the letter, whose praise is not from men, but from God.[76]

But as God has distributed to every man, as the Lord has called each one, so let him walk. And this is what I ordain in all the churches. Is any man called while being circumcised? Let him not seek to become uncircumcised. Is anyone called while uncircumcised? Let him not become circumcised. Circumcision is nothing, and uncircumcision is nothing, but what counts is the keeping of God's commandments.[77]

THE CONDITION
OF ALL MEN

Wat advantage does the Jew have then? Or
what profit is there in circumcision? Much
every way——chiefly because to them the
oracles of God were committed. What if some did not
believe? Shall their unbelief nullify the faith of God? God
forbid. Yes, let God be true, but every man a liar, as it is
written, "That you might be justified in your sayings, and
might overcome when you are judged." But if our unrighteousness commends the righteousness of God, what
can we say in response? Is God unrighteous if He takes
vengeance? (I speak on a human level.) God forbid——for
how then could God judge the world? For if the truth of
God abounds to His glory through my lie, then why am
I judged as a sinner? And why not instead say (as some
slanderously report that we do, as some affirm that we
say), "Let us do evil, that good may come of it"? Their
damnation is just. So what then? Are we better than they
are? No, not at all. We have already proved that Jews and
Gentiles are together under sin. As it is written, "There is
no one righteous, no, not even one. There is no one who
understands, there is no one who seeks after God. They
have all gone out of the way, they have together become
unprofitable; there is none that does good, no, not one.

Their throat is an open sepulcher; with their tongues they have used deceit; the poison of asps is under their lips. Their mouth is full of cursing and bitterness. Their feet are swift to shed blood, destruction and misery are in their ways, and the way of peace they have not known. There is no fear of God before their eyes.[78]

Knowing that a man is not justified by the works of the law, but rather by the faith of Jesus Christ, we have therefore believed in Jesus Christ, so that we might be justified by the faith of Christ, and not by the works of the law. For by the works of the law no flesh shall ever be justified. Now if——while we seek to be justified by Christ——we ourselves are shown to be sinners, is Christ therefore the minister of sin? God forbid it. For if I rebuild the things which I earlier destroyed, I make myself the transgressor. For through the law I am dead to the law, in order that I might live to God. I have been crucified with Christ, nevertheless I live. Yet not I, but Christ lives in me——and the life which I now live in the flesh I live by the faith of the Son of God, who loved me, and gave Himself up for me. I do not frustrate the grace of God, for if righteousness comes by the law, then Christ died in vain.[79]

Now we know that whatever things the law says, it says it to those who are under the law, so that every mouth might be stopped, and the whole world might become guilty before God. Therefore no flesh will be justified in His sight by the deeds of the law, for by the law is the knowledge of sin. But now the righteousness of God apart from the law is manifested, being witnessed by the law and the prophets, by which I mean the righteousness of God by the faith of Jesus Christ to all and upon all those who believe, for there is no difference. For all have sinned and fallen short of the glory of God, and are justified freely by His grace through the redemption that is in Christ Jesus. He is the one whom God has set forth to be a propitiation through faith in His blood, to declare His righteousness for the remission of past sins, through the forbearance of God. I say He does this to declare His righteousness at this time, so that He might both be just and the One who justifies the one who believes in Jesus. Where is boasting then? It is excluded. By what law? The law of works? No, but rather by the law of faith. That is why we conclude that a man is justified by faith apart from deeds of the law. Is God the God of the Jews only? Is He not also God of the Gentiles? Yes, of the Gentiles also——seeing there is only one God, who shall justify the circumcised by faith, and the uncircumcised also through faith. Do we then make void the law through faith? God forbid——rather we establish the law.[80]

And you He has made alive who were dead in trespasses and sins, which in previous times you walked in accordance with the course of this world, according to the prince of the power of the air, the spirit who now works in the children of disobedience, among whom we all had our way of life in time past——in the lusts of our flesh, fulfilling the desires of the flesh and of the mind, and were by nature children of wrath, even as others are.[81]

But after the kindness and love of God our Savior toward man appeared——not by works of righteousness which we have done, but according to His mercy——He saved us. He did this by the washing of regeneration, and the renewing of the Holy Ghost, which He shed on us abundantly through Jesus Christ our Savior. He did this so that, being justified by His grace, we should be made heirs in accordance with the hope of eternal life. This is a faithful saying, and these things I want you to affirm constantly, so that those who have believed in God might be careful to maintain good works. These things are good and profitable for men. But avoid foolish questions, and genealogies, and contentions, and strivings over the law, which are unprofitable and vain. Reject a man who is a heretic after the first and second admonition, knowing that such men are subverted, and they sin as self-condemned.[82]

For Christ did not send me to baptize, but rather to preach the gospel——and not with wisdom of words either——lest the cross of Christ be made of no effect. For the preaching of the cross is foolishness to those who are perishing, but to us who are saved it is the power of God. For it is written, "I will destroy the wisdom of the wise, and will bring to nothing the understanding of the discerning. Where is the wise? Where is the scribe? Where is the debater of this age? Has not God made foolish the wisdom of this world? For in the wisdom of God the world through its wisdom did not know God, it pleased God by the foolishness of preaching to save those who believe. For the Jews require a sign, and the Greeks seek after wisdom——but we preach Christ crucified, to the Jews a stumbling block, and to the Greeks foolishness. But to those who are called, both Jews and Greeks, Christ is the power of God, and the wisdom of God. This is because the foolishness of God is wiser than men, and the weakness of God is stronger than men. For you see your calling, brothers, how not many of you were called as wise men after the flesh, not many mighty, not many noble.

But God has chosen the foolish things of the world in order to confound the wise; and God has chosen the weak things of the world in order to confound the things which are mighty. And He has chosen the contemptible things of the world, things which are despised——yes, things which are nothing——in order to bring to nothing things of substance, so that no flesh might glory in His presence. But you are of Him in Christ Jesus, who of God is made to us wisdom, and righteousness, and sanctification, and redemption. This is so that, according to what is written, "He that glories, let him glory in the Lord."[83]

The Holy Spirit spoke well through Isaiah the prophet to our fathers, saying, "Go to this people and say, 'Hearing you will hear, but will not understand, and seeing you will see, but not perceive. For the heart of this people has grown thick, and their ears can scarcely hear, and they have closed their eyes——lest they should see with their eyes, and hear with their ears, and understand with their heart, and should turn, and I would heal them.'"

Therefore let it be known to you that the salvation of God is now sent to the Gentiles——and they will listen to it.[84]

It was necessary that the word of God should be spoken to you first. But seeing that you put it away from you, and judge yourselves unworthy of everlasting life, then consider. We turn to the Gentiles. For thus the Lord has commanded us, saying, "I have set you to be a light for the Gentiles, that you should be for salvation to the ends of the earth."[85]

May your blood be upon your own heads; I am clean. From this time on I will go to the Gentiles.[86]

Believe on the Lord Jesus Christ, and you will be saved, you and your household.[87]

This Jesus, whom I preach to you, is Christ.[88]

FATHER ABRAHAM

What shall we then say that our father Abraham, as far as the flesh is concerned, has found? For if Abraham was justified by works, he had something to glory in——but not before God. For what does Scripture say? Abraham believed God, and it was counted unto him for righteousness. Now to the one who works, the reward is not reckoned as grace, but rather as debt. But to the one who does not work, but believes on Him who justifies the ungodly, his faith is counted for righteousness. Even as David also describes the blessedness of the man to whom God imputes righteousness apart from works, saying, Blessed are those whose iniquities are forgiven, and whose sins are covered. Blessed is the man to whom the Lord does not impute sin.

Does this blessedness then come upon the circumcised only, or upon the uncircumcised also? For we say that *faith* was reckoned to Abraham for righteousness. How was it then reckoned? Was it reckoned when he was circumcised, or when uncircumcised? Not while he was circumcised, but rather when he was uncircumcised. And he received the sign of circumcision, a seal of the righteousness of the faith which he had when he was still uncircumcised, so that he might be the father of all those who believe, even though they are not circumcised, that righteousness might be imputed to them as well. This is so that he might be the father of the circumcised to those who are not merely circumcised, but who also walk in the steps of the faith of our father Abraham, which he had when still uncircumcised.

For the promise that he would be heir of the world was not given to Abraham, or to his seed, through the law, but through the righteousness of faith. For if those who are of the law are heirs, then faith is made void and the promise is made of no effect, This is because the law works wrath, and where there is no law, there is also no transgression. This is why it is of faith, so that it might be by grace——to the end that the promise might be made sure to all the seed, not only to those who are of the law, but also to those who are of the faith of Abraham, who is the father of us all, As it is written, "I have made thee a father of many nations," and so before Him whom he believed, even God, who quickens the dead, and calls those things which are not as though they were. Who against hope believed, in hope, in order that he might become the father of many nations, according to that which was spoken, "So shall thy seed be." And not being weak in faith, he did not reckon his own body as dead, when he was about an hundred years old, nor yet the deadness of Sara's womb. He did not stagger in unbelief at the promise of God, but was strong in faith, giving glory to God.

He was fully persuaded that what God had promised He was also able to perform. And so it was therefore imputed to him for righteousness. Now it was not just for his sake alone that it was written that "it was imputed" to him, but for us also, to whom it shall also be imputed, provided we believe in Him who raised up Jesus our Lord from the dead. He was delivered up for our offenses, and was raised again for our justification.[89]

THE CURSE OF THE LAW

Therefore having been justified by faith, we have peace with God through our Lord Jesus Christ——by whom we also have access by faith into this grace in which we stand, and we rejoice in hope of the glory of God. And not only so, but we glory in our tribulations also, knowing that tribulation works patience; and patience, experience; and experience, hope. And hope does not leave us ashamed because the love of God is shed abroad in our hearts by the Holy Spirit, who is given to us.[90]

But God, who is rich in mercy, through His great love with which He loved us, has made us alive together with Christ even though we were dead in sins——by grace you are saved——and has raised us up together, and has made us sit together in the heavenly places in Christ Jesus. He did this so that in the ages to come He might manifest the exceeding riches of His grace in His kindness toward us through Christ Jesus. For by grace you are saved through faith, and that is not of yourselves——it is the gift of God, not by works, lest any man should boast. For we are His workmanship, created in Christ Jesus for good works, which God has ordained beforehand so that we might walk in them.[91]

And this is so I might be found in Him, not having my own righteousness——which is of the law——but that which is through the faith of Christ, the righteousness which is of God by faith. This is so that I may know Him and the power of His resurrection, and the fellowship of His sufferings, being made conformable unto His death——if by any means I might attain to the resurrection of the dead. Not as though I had already attained it, or were already perfect, but I pursue after it, so that I might apprehend that for which I was also apprehended by Christ Jesus.[92]

For the grace of God that brings salvation has appeared to all men, teaching us that——denying ungodliness and worldly lusts——we should live sober, righteous, and godly lives in this present world, as we look for that blessed hope, the glorious appearing of the great God and our Savior Jesus Christ, who gave Himself for us so that He might redeem us from all iniquity, purifying us to Himself as a peculiar people, zealous for good works. Speak these things, and exhort and rebuke with all authority. Let no man despise you.[93]

For when we had no strength, at the right time, Christ died for the ungodly. Now someone might die for a righteous man; it is possible that someone would dare to die for a good man. But God commends His love to us, in that, while we were still sinners, Christ died for us. That being the case, how much more, being justified now by His blood, will we be saved from wrath through Him? For if——while we were still enemies——we were reconciled to God through the death of His Son, how much more, being reconciled, we will be saved by His life. And not only this, but we also rejoice in God through our Lord Jesus Christ, through whom we have now received this atonement. For as by one man sin entered the world, and death through sin, and so it was that death passed to all men, for all have sinned.

For until the time of the law, sin was in the world, but sin is not imputed when there is no law. At the same time, death reigned from Adam to Moses, even over those who had not sinned according to the likeness of Adam's transgression——who is the figure of Him who was to come. And the free gift is not like the offense. For if through the offense of one man, many are dead, how much more the grace of God and the gift by grace, through one man, Jesus Christ, has abounded for many. And unlike the one who sinned, the gift differs. For the judgment came by one resulting in condemnation, but the free gift followed many offenses and resulted in justification. For if by one man's offense death reigned by that one man, how much more will another one, Jesus Christ, bring abundance of grace and the gift of righteousness to reign in life. Therefore as the offense of one man brought judgment upon all men to condemnation, even so by the righteousness of one man the free gift came to all men for justification of life. For just as by one man's disobedience many were made sinners, so also by the obedience of one shall many be made righteous. Moreover the reason the law entered was so that the offense might abound. But where sin abounded, grace abounded much more. As sin has reigned to the point of death, even so grace will reign through righteousness unto eternal life by Jesus Christ our Lord.[94]

O you foolish Galatians, who has bewitched you to not obey the truth? Before your eyes Jesus Christ was obviously presented, crucified before you. This one thing I would learn from you——did you receive the Spirit by works of the law, or by hearing with faith? Are you so foolish? Having begun in the Spirit, are you now made complete through the flesh? Have you suffered so many things in vain? Perhaps it is not yet in vain. He that ministers the Spirit to you, and works miracles among you, does He do it by works of the law, or by hearing with faith? It was just this way that Abraham believed God, and it was reckoned to him for righteousness. You must know therefore that those who are of faith, the same are the children of Abraham. And the Scripture, foreseeing that God would justify the Gentiles through faith, preached the gospel to Abraham beforehand, saying, "In you all nations shall be blessed." So then those who are of faith are blessed along with faithful Abraham. For as many as are of the works of the law are under the curse, for it is written, "Cursed is everyone who continues not in all things which are written in the book of the law to do them." But that no man can be justified by the law in the sight of God is evident, as it says, "The just shall live by faith." And the law is not according to faith but rather, "The man who *does* them shall live in them."

Christ has redeemed us from the curse of the law, having been made a curse for us. As it is written, "Cursed is everyone who is hanged on a tree"——that the blessing of Abraham might come to the Gentiles through Jesus Christ, that we might receive the promise of the Spirit through faith. Brothers, I speak according to the manner of men. Though it is only a human covenant, and it is finalized, no one set it aside, or adds to it. Now the promises were made to Abraham and his seed. He does not say, "And to *seeds*," as of many, but concerning one, "And to your seed," which is Christ. And so I say this——the covenant, which was confirmed beforehand by God in Christ, could not be disannulled by the law, which came four hundred and thirty years later, in such a way as to make the promise of no effect. For if the inheritance comes through the law, it is not a promise anymore. But God gave it to Abraham by a *promise*.

What then is the point of the law? It was added because of transgressions, until the seed should come to whom the promise was made; and it was ordained by angels through the hand of a mediator. Now a mediator is not a mediator when there is only one, but God is one. Is the law therefore against the promises of God? God forbid. For if there had been a law given which could have given life, then in truth righteousness would have been through the law. But in fact Scripture has settled all under sin, so that the promise through the faith of Jesus Christ might be given to those who believe. But before that faith came, we were kept under the law, shut up and waiting for the faith which should afterwards be revealed. This is why the law was our schoolmaster to bring us to Christ, so that we might be justified by faith. But once that faith has come, we are no longer under a schoolmaster.

For you are all the children of God through faith in Christ Jesus. For as many of you as have been baptized into Christ have put on Christ. There is neither Jew nor Greek, there is neither bond nor free, there is neither male nor female: for you are all one in Christ Jesus. And if you are Christ's, then you are Abraham's seed, and heirs according to the promise.[95]

INTO HIS DEATH

What shall we say then? Shall we continue in sin so that grace may abound? God forbid it. How shall we who are dead to sin live in it any longer? Do you not know that as many of us as were baptized into Jesus Christ were baptized into His death? Therefore we are buried with Him by baptism into death, so that just as Christ was raised up from the dead by the glory of the Father, even so we also should walk in newness of life. For if we have been planted together in the likeness of His death, we shall also be planted in the likeness of His resurrection——knowing this, that our old man is crucified with Him, so that the body of sin might be destroyed, and that from that point we should no longer serve sin. For he who is dead is freed from sin. Now if we are dead with Christ, we believe that we shall also live with Him, knowing that Christ, having been raised from the dead, dies no more. Death has no more dominion over Him.

For in that He died, He died unto sin once, but in that He lives, He lives unto God. In the same way, you also reckon yourselves to be dead to sin, but alive to God through Jesus Christ our Lord. Therefore do not let sin reign in your mortal body, that you should obey it in its lusts. Neither present your members to sin as instruments of unrighteousness, but present yourselves unto God, as those who are alive from the dead, and your members as instruments of righteousness unto God. For sin shall not have dominion over you——for you are not under the law, but under grace. What then? Shall we sin because we are not under the law, but under grace? God forbid it. Do you not know that you are the slaves of the one to whom you yield yourselves as slaves to obey——you are slaves of the one you *obey*. Do you not know it is either sin unto death, or obedience unto righteousness?

But God be thanked, that though you were slaves of sin, you have obeyed that form of doctrine which was delivered to you from the heart. Being then set free from sin, you became slaves of righteousness. I speak according to the custom of men because of the weakness of your flesh——for as you yielded your members as slaves of uncleanness and ever-increasing iniquity, even so now you must yield your members as slaves to righteousness ending in holiness. For when you were slaves of sin, you were free from righteousness. What fruit did you bear then in those things you are now ashamed of? The end of such things is death. But now, set free from sin, you have become slaves of God, and you bear your fruit unto holiness, and the result of everlasting life. For the wages of sin is death; but the gift of God is eternal life through Jesus Christ our Lord.[96]

For those who desire to make a fair showing in the flesh constrain you to be circumcised——lest *they* suffer persecution for the sake of the cross of Christ. For those who are themselves circumcised do not keep the law, but simply desire to have *you* circumcised, in order that they may glory in your flesh. But God forbid that I should glory except in the cross of our Lord Jesus Christ, by whom the world is crucified to me, and I to the world. For in Christ Jesus neither circumcision nor lack of circumcision avails anything, but rather a new creature.[97]

Now we know that if this tent of our earthly home is dissolved, we have a building of God, a house not made with hands, eternal in the heavens. For in this state we groan, earnestly desiring to be clothed with our home which is from heaven, so that when we are clothed we will not be found naked. For those of us who are in this tent groan, under a burden——not that we want to be unclothed, but rather clothed, so that mortality might be swallowed up by life. Now He who has fashioned us for this very thing is God, who also has given to us the earnest payment of the Spirit. Therefore we are always confident, knowing that while we are at home in the body we are absent from the Lord. For we walk by faith, and not by sight. We are confident, I say, and would rather be absent from the body, and so present with the Lord.

Therefore we labor in order that, whether present or absent, we may be accepted by Him. For we must all appear before the judgment seat of Christ, so that everyone may receive back the things done in his body, according to what he has done, whether good or bad. Knowing therefore the fear of the Lord, we persuade men——but we are made manifest before God, and I trust we are also made manifest in your consciences. For we do not commend ourselves again to you, but rather give you opportunity to glory on our behalf, so that you may have something to answer those who glory in appearances, and not in the heart. For if we are beside ourselves, it is for God, but if we are sober, it is for your sake. For the love of Christ constrains us, because this is how we judge, that if one died for all, then all are dead. And He died for all so that they who live should not live for themselves from that point, but for Him who died for them and rose again.

Because of this, we no longer know any man according to the flesh——yes, even though we once knew Christ according to the flesh, we now no longer know Him this way. Therefore if any man is in Christ, he is a new creation. Old things have passed away, and behold, all things have become new. And all things are of God, who has reconciled us to Himself by Jesus Christ, and has given to us the ministry of reconciliation——that is, that God was in Christ, reconciling the world to Himself, not imputing their trespasses to them. And He has committed unto us the word of reconciliation. So then we are ambassadors for Christ, as though God were beseeching you through us. We plead with you, for Christ's sake, be reconciled to God. For He has made Him to be sin for us, who knew no sin, so that in Him we might be made the righteousness of God.[98]

Beware lest any man ruin you through philosophy and vain deceit, according to the tradition of men, according to the rudiments of this world, and not after Christ. For in Him all the fullness of the Godhead dwells bodily. And you are complete in Him, who is the head over all principality and power——in whom you also are circumcised with the circumcision done without hands, in putting off the body of the sins of the flesh by the circumcision of Christ. You were buried with Him in baptism, in which you were also raised with Him through faith in the work of God, who has raised Him from the dead. And you, being dead in your sins and in the uncircumcision of your flesh, He has made alive together with Him, having forgiven you all your trespasses. He blotted out the handwritten script of ordinances that was against us, which was contrary to us, and took it out of the way, nailing it to His cross. And having pillaged the principalities and powers, He made an open spectacle of them, triumphing over them in it.[99]

Now I, Paul myself, a man who is contemptible when with you and bold when away from you, plead with you by the meekness and gentleness of Christ. I plead with you, so that I will not have to be bold when I am present with you with the kind of confidence which I need to have with some——those who think of us as though we walked according to the flesh. For though we *walk* in the flesh, we do not conduct our warfare after the flesh. The weapons of our warfare are not carnal, but rather mighty through God to the pulling down of strongholds——casting down imaginations, and every high thing that exalts itself against the knowledge of God, and bringing every thought into captivity, to the obedience of Christ, and being quite ready to deal with all disobedience, when your obedience is complete.[100]

DRIVEN TO CHRIST

D o you not know, brothers——I am speaking to those who know the law——how the law has dominion over a man as long as he lives? For the woman who has a husband is bound by the law to her husband as long as he lives. But if the husband is dead, she is freed from the law of her husband. So then if, while her husband lives, she gets married to another man, she will be called an adulteress. But if her husband is dead, she is free from that law, meaning that she is no adulteress, even though she is married to another man. Therefore, my brothers, you also are dead to the law through the body of Christ——so that you might be married to another, even to Him who was raised from the dead, so that we might bring forth fruit to God. For when we were in the flesh, the stirring of sin, which arose from the law, worked in our members to bring forth fruit to death. But now we are delivered from the law, being dead to what once bound us, so that we might serve in newness of spirit, and not in the oldness of the letter.

What shall we say then? Is the law sin? God forbid it. No, I would not have known sin except through the law. I would not have known lust unless the law had said, "You shall not covet." But sin, taking the occasion created by the commandment, worked in me all kinds of desires. For apart from the law sin is dead. For once I was alive apart from the law, but when the commandment arrived, sin revived and I died. And the commandment, which was intended for life, I found to be unto death. For sin, taking the occasion created by the commandment, deceived me, and by the law killed me. Therefore the law is holy, and the commandment is holy, righteous, and good. Was this good thing therefore death to me? God forbid it. But sin, in order to appear as sin, worked death in me by means of that which is good——so that sin (by means of the commandment) might become exceedingly sinful.

For we know that the law is spiritual but I am carnal, sold under sin. For that which I do I would not do. And what I would do, that I don't do. And what I hate, that is what I do. If then I do what I would not do, I consent to the law, acknowledging that it is good. Now then, it is no longer I who am doing it, but rather the sin that dwells in me. For I know that in me——that is, in my flesh——dwells no good thing. For the will to do good is present in me, but how to *do* what is good I cannot find. For the good that I will, I do not do, but the evil which I would not do, I wind up doing. Now if I do what I do not wish to do, it is no longer I who is doing it, but rather sin that dwells in me. I find within me a law that requires——when I want to do good——evil is still present with me. For I delight in the law of God in the inward man——but I see another law in my members, warring against the law of my mind, and bringing me into captivity to the law of sin which is in my members.[101]

This is what I say then——walk in the Spirit, and you will not fulfill the lusts of the flesh. For the flesh lusts against the Spirit, and the Spirit against the flesh, and these two are contrary to one another to keep you from doing what you would do. But if you are led by the Spirit, you are not under the law. Now the works of the flesh are manifest, which are as follows: adultery, fornication, uncleanness, sensuality, idolatry, witchcraft, hatred, strife, jealousy, fits of wrath, rivalry, disputes, factions, envy, murders, drunkenness, raves, and such things. I warn you, as I have before, that those who do such things will not inherit the kingdom of God.

But the fruit of the Spirit is love, joy, peace, patience, kindness, goodness, faithfulness, gentleness, self-control——against such things there is no law. And those who belong to Christ have crucified the flesh with its passions and lusts. If we live by the Spirit, let us also stay in step with the Spirit. Let us not desire vainglory, provoking one another, envying one another.[102]

O wretched man that I am! So who shall deliver me from this body of death? I thank God through Jesus Christ our Lord. So then with the mind I do serve the law of God——but with the flesh the law of sin.[103]

ABBA, FATHER

T herefore there is now no condemnation for those who are in Christ Jesus, who do not walk after the flesh, but rather after the Spirit. For the law of the Spirit of life in Christ Jesus has set me free from the law of sin and death. For what the law could not do, being weak on account of the flesh, God did by sending His own Son in the appearance of sinful flesh and for sin, He condemned sin in the flesh. He did this so that the righteousness of the law might be fulfilled in us, who do walk not after the flesh, but after the Spirit. For those who are according to the flesh are mindful of the things of the flesh, but those who are according to the Spirit mind the things of the Spirit. For to be carnally-minded is death, but to be spiritually-minded is life and peace. The carnal mind is enmity against God——it is not subject to the law of God, and indeed neither can it be. So then those who are in the flesh cannot please God. But you are not in the flesh, but in the Spirit, if in fact the Spirit of God dwells in you. And if any man does not have the Spirit of Christ, he does not belong to Him.

And if Christ is in you, the body is dead because of sin but the Spirit is life because of righteousness. If the Spirit of Him who raised up Jesus from the dead dwells in you, He who raised up Christ from the dead will also make alive your mortal bodies by His Spirit who dwells in you.

Therefore, brothers, we are debtors——but not to the flesh, to live according to the flesh. For if you live according to the flesh, you will die, but if through the Spirit you mortify the deeds of the body, you will live. For as many as are led by the Spirit of God, these are the sons of God. For you have not received the spirit of bondage again to fear, but rather you have received the Spirit of adoption, by which we cry, *Abba, Father*. The Spirit Himself bears witness with our spirit that we are the children of God.[104]

So if you are then raised with Christ, then seek those things which are above, where Christ sits at the right hand of God. Set your affection on things above, and not on things on earth. For you are dead, and your life is hidden with Christ in God. When Christ who is our life appears, then you also will appear with Him in glory.

Therefore put to death your members which are upon the earth——by which I mean fornication, impurity, passion, corrupt desires and covetousness, which is idolatry. On account of such things the wrath of God is coming upon the children of disobedience. In these things you used to walk, when that was your life. But now you must put all these things away: anger, wrath, malice, slander, and corrupt talk in your mouth. Do not lie to one another, seeing that you have put off the old man together with his deeds, and have put on the new man, which is being renewed in knowledge according to the image of its creator. In this there is not Greek or Jew, circumcision or uncircumcision, barbarian, Scythian, slave or free——but Christ is all, and in all.

Therefore, as the elect of God, holy and beloved, put on compassionate mercies, kindness, humility of mind, meekness, and patience, bearing with one another, and if anyone has a complaint against another, forgiving one another. Even as Christ forgave you, so also you must forgive. And above all these things, put on love, which binds all things in perfect harmony. And let the peace of God rule in your hearts, to which you were also called in one body——and be thankful. Let the Word of Christ dwell in you richly in all wisdom, teaching and admonishing one another in psalms and hymns and spiritual songs, singing with grace in your hearts to the Lord. And whatever you do in word or deed, do it all in the name of the Lord Jesus, giving thanks to our God and Father by Him.[105]

Now if we are children, then we are heirs——heirs of God and joint-heirs together with Christ. If we suffer with Him, then we may be glorified together with Him. For I consider that the sufferings of this present time are not worthy to be compared with the glory which shall be revealed in us. For the earnest expectation of the creation waits for the manifestation of the sons of God. The creation was subjected to vanity, not voluntarily, but by the plan of Him who subjected it in hope——because the creation itself will also be delivered from its bondage to corruption into the glorious liberty of the children of God.

For we know that the whole creation groans and travails in pain together until the present. And not only the creation, but we also, who have the first fruits of the Spirit——we also groan in ourselves, waiting for our adoption, that is, the redemption of our body. For we are saved in hope, but hope that is seen is not really hope. For if a man sees it, why is he still hoping? But if we hope for what we do not see, then we patiently wait for it.[106]

Now you who are troubled may rest with us, when the Lord Jesus shall be revealed from heaven with His mighty angels. He will come in flaming fire to take vengeance on those who do not know God, and who do not obey the gospel of our Lord Jesus Christ. They will be punished with everlasting destruction away from the presence of the Lord, and away from the glory of His power. This will happen when He will come to be glorified in His saints, and to be marveled at by all those who believe in that day. I say this because our testimony among you *was* believed.[107]

Now we plead with you, brothers, by the coming of our Lord Jesus Christ, and by our gathering together to Him, not to be quickly shaken in mind, or otherwise troubled, whether by spirit, or by word, or by a purported letter from us, saying that the day of Christ is at hand. Let no man deceive you by any means. That day will not come unless there is an apostasy first, and the man of sin is revealed——the son of perdition. He is the one who opposes and exalts himself above anything that is called God, or that is worshipped. So he sits as God in the temple of

God, representing himself *as* God. Do you not remember how I told you these things when I was with you?

And now you know what is restraining him, so that he might be revealed in his own time. For the mystery of iniquity is already at work, but he who now restrains will continue, until he is taken out of the way. And then shall that lawless one be revealed, whom the Lord will consume with the spirit of His mouth, destroying him with the brightness of His coming. This is the one, even the one whose coming is according to the working of Satan, with all power and signs and lying wonders, and with all wicked deceits for those who are perishing——because they did not receive a love of the truth, so that they might be saved. And for this reason God will send them a strong delusion so that they would believe a lie——so that they might all be damned who did not believe the truth, but took pleasure in unrighteousness.[108]

Brothers, I plead with you, be as I am, for I am as you are. You have not injured me at all. You know how it was through an infirmity of the flesh that I preached the gospel to you in the first place. And you did not despise my trial in my flesh, and did not reject me, but rather received me as an angel of God, even as Christ Jesus. Where now is the blessedness you used to speak of? For I can testify that, had it been possible, you would have plucked out your own eyes in order to give them to me. How have I become your enemy by telling you the truth? They zealously make much of you, but not for good reasons. They shut you out, so that you might fawn over them. It is good to be made much of for a good reason, and not only when I am present with you. My little children, for whom I am in pangs of childbirth again until Christ is formed in you. My desire is to be present with you now, and to change my tone——for I am doubtful about you.[109]

A GROANING WORLD

In the same way, the Spirit helps us in our infirmities, for we do not know how to pray as we ought to. But the Spirit Himself makes intercession for us with groans that cannot be uttered. And He who searches the hearts knows the mind of the Spirit because He makes intercession for the saints according to the will of God. And we know that all things work together for good for those who love God, to those who are the called according to His purpose.

For those whom He foreknew, He predestined to be conformed to the image of His Son, so that He might be the firstborn among many brothers. And moreover, those whom He predestined, those He also called. And those whom He called, those He also justified, and those He justified, He also glorified.

What then shall we say to these things? If God is for us, who can be against us? He who did not spare His own Son, but delivered Him up for us all——how will He not freely give us all things together with Him? Who will lay a charge against God's elect? It is God who justifies. Who is he that condemns? It is *Christ* who died——in fact who is risen again, and who is even now at the right hand of God, also making intercession for us. What will separate us from the love of Christ? Will it be tribulation, or distress, or persecution, or famine, or nakedness, or peril, or sword? As it is written, "For your sake we are killed all the day long; we are accounted as sheep for the slaughter." No——in all these things we are more than conquerors through Him who loved us. For I am persuaded that neither death, nor life, nor angels, nor principalities, nor powers, nor things present, nor things to come, nor height, nor depth, nor any other created thing, will be able to separate us from the love of God, which is in Christ Jesus our Lord.[110]

For truly, when we were with you before, we told you that we would suffer tribulation——even as it came to pass, as you know. For this reason, when I could no longer stand it, I sent to find out about your faith, lest in some fashion the tempter may have tempted you, and all our labor be in vain. But now that Timothy came to us from you, and brought us good news about your faith and love, and that you have good memories of us always, desiring greatly to see us, as we also to see you, then it was, brothers, that we were comforted over you concerning your faith in all our affliction and distress. For now we live, if you stand fast in the Lord. For what thanks can we render again to God for you? For all the joy that we rejoice in for your sakes before our God? Night and day we have prayed intensely that we might see your face, and might make complete that which is lacking in your faith.

Now may God Himself, our Father, and our Lord Jesus Christ, direct our way unto you. And may the Lord make you to increase and abound in love one toward another, and toward all men, even as we do toward you. This would be to the end that He might establish your hearts blameless in holiness before God, even our Father, at the coming of our Lord Jesus Christ, together with all His saints.[111]

For this reason I bow my knees before the Father of our Lord Jesus Christ, from whom all fatherhood in heaven and earth derives its name. I have prayed that He would grant you, according to the riches of His glory, to be strengthened with might by His Spirit in the inner man, so that Christ might dwell in your hearts by faith. The result would be that you, being rooted and grounded in love, might be able to comprehend with all saints what is the breadth, and length, and depth, and height, and also to know the love of Christ, which passes knowledge, that you might be filled with all the fullness of God.

Now unto Him who is able to do exceeding abundantly above all that we ask or think, according to the power that works in us, unto Him be glory in the church by Christ Jesus throughout all ages, world without end. Amen.[112]

Brothers, I do not count myself to have apprehended this. But this one thing I do——I forget those things that are behind, and I reach forward to those things which are ahead. I press on toward the mark of the prize of the high calling of God in Christ Jesus. Therefore let us, as many as are mature, have this mind. And if in anything you are otherwise minded, God will reveal this to you. Nevertheless, let us live up to what we have already attained. Let us walk by the same rule, let us have the same mind.

Brothers, join together to imitate me, and notice those who walk with us as an example. For there are many who walk——as I have told you often, and tell you again with tears——as enemies of the cross of Christ. Their end is destruction, their god is their belly, and their glory is in their shame. They set their mind on earthly things. But our citizenship is in heaven, and from there we look for our Savior, the Lord Jesus Christ. He will change our vile body so that it might be fashioned to the pattern of His glorious body, according to the work by which He is able to subdue all things to Himself.[113]

You know, from the first day that I came into Asia, what my manner has been with you in all seasons. I have served the Lord with all humility of mind, and with many tears and trials which befell me through the plots of the Jews. And you know how I held back nothing that would be profitable to you, but how I have showed you, and have taught you publicly, even from house to house. You know how I testified to both Jews and Greeks, teaching repentance toward God and faith toward our Lord Jesus Christ.

And now, consider, bound in spirit I go to Jerusalem, not knowing what things will befall me there——except that the Holy Spirit testifies in every city that bonds and afflictions await me. But none of this moves me. I do not count my life dear to myself so that I might finish my race with joy, along with my ministry, which I have received from the Lord Jesus, which is to testify the gospel of the grace of God. And now, consider, I know that all of you, among whom I have gone preaching the kingdom of God, shall not see my face anymore. That is why I call you to witness this day that I am innocent of the blood of all men. For I have not neglected to declare to you the entire counsel of God. Therefore pay attention to yourselves, and to the whole flock——over which the Holy Spirit has made you overseers——to feed the church of God, which He has purchased with His own blood. For I know this—— after my departure grievous wolves will enter in among you, not sparing the flock. And also men will arise out of your own ranks, speaking perverse things, in order to draw disciples away after them.

Therefore watch, and recall that for the space of three years I did not cease to warn everyone night and day with tears. So now, brothers, I commend you to God, and to the word of His grace, which is able to build you up, and to give you an inheritance among all those who are sanctified. I have coveted no man's silver or gold or clothing. Yes, you yourselves know that these hands have provided my own necessities, as well as those who were with me. I have showed you in all things, how in laboring this way you ought to support the weak, and to remember the words of the Lord Jesus——recall that He said, "It is more blessed to give than to receive."[114]

I would not have you ignorant, brothers, concerning those who are asleep. Do not sorrow the way others do, who have no hope. For if we believe that Jesus died and rose again, even so those also who are asleep in Jesus will God bring with Him. For we tell you this, by the word of the Lord, that those of us who are alive and remain until the coming of the Lord will not go ahead of those who are asleep. For the Lord Himself will descend from heaven with a shout, with the voice of the archangel, and with the trumpet of God. And the dead in Christ will rise first, and *then* those who are alive and remain shall be caught up together with them in the clouds, to meet the Lord in the air. And so we will be with the Lord forever. Therefore comfort each other with these words.

Of the times and the seasons, brothers, you have no need for me to write to you. For you know perfectly well that the day of the Lord will come as a thief in the night. For when they all say, "Peace and safety," then sudden destruction will come upon them, the way birth pangs come upon a pregnant woman, and they will not escape. But you, brothers, are not in darkness, such that this day should overtake you like a thief. You are all children of light, and children of the day——we are not of the night, nor are we of darkness.

Therefore do not sleep, the way others do, but rather let us watch and be sober. For those who sleep do so at night. And those who are drunk get drunk at night. But let us be sober. We are of the day. Put on the breastplate of faith and love, and the hope of salvation for a helmet. For God has not appointed us to wrath, but rather to obtain salvation by our Lord Jesus Christ. He died for us so that, whether we wake or sleep, we should live together with Him. Therefore comfort yourselves together, and edify one another, even as you are already doing.[115]

MY UNBELIEVING
KINSMEN

I tell you the truth in Christ, I am not lying. My conscience also bears me witness in the Holy Spirit, that I have great heaviness and continual sorrow in my heart. For I could even wish that I were accursed from Christ for the sake of my brothers, my kinsmen in the flesh. I mean the Israelites, to whom pertain the adoption, and the glory, and the covenants, and the giving of the law, and the worship of God, and the promises. Theirs are the fathers, and from whom——according to the flesh——Christ came, who is over all, God blessed forever. Amen.

It is not as though the Word of God had taken no effect. For they are not all Israel who are *of* Israel. Neither are they all children just because they are the seed of Abraham, but rather, "In Isaac will your seed be called." So then, those who are the children of the flesh are not the children of God, but the children of the promise are reckoned as the seed. For this is the word of promise, "At this time I will come, and Sara will have a son." And not only so, but when Rebecca also had conceived by one man, even by our father Isaac——with the children not yet born, not having done any good or evil, so that the purpose of God according to election might stand, not of works, but of Him who calls——it was said to her, "The elder shall serve the younger." As it is written, "Jacob I have loved, but Esau I hated."

What then shall we say? Is God unrighteousness? God forbid it. For He says to Moses, "I will have mercy on whom I will have mercy, and I will have compassion on whom I will have compassion." So then it is not of him who wills, nor of him who runs, but of God who shows mercy. For the Scripture says to Pharaoh, "For this very purpose I raised you up, in order to show my power in you, and so that my name might be declared throughout all the earth." Therefore He has mercy on whom He will have mercy, and He hardens whom He wills. You will then say to me——why does He then find fault? For who can resist His will? No, little man. Who are you to reply against God? Shall the thing formed say to him who formed it, "Why did you make me like this?" Does not the potter have power over the clay, out of the same lump, to make one vessel for honor and another for dishonor?

What if God, wanting to show His wrath, and to make His power known, endured with much patience the vessels of wrath fitted for destruction? What if He did this to make known the riches of His glory on the vessels of mercy, which He had beforehand prepared for glory? I mean us, even us, whom He has called, not from the Jews only, but also from the Gentiles.

As He says also in Hosea, "I will call them my people who were not my people, and call her beloved who was not beloved." And it will come to pass that in the place where it was said to them, "You are not my people," there they will be called "children of the living God."

Isaiah also cries out concerning Israel, "Though the number of the children of Israel be as the sand of the sea, only a remnant shall be saved. For He will finish the work and cut it short in righteousness——because the Lord will make a short work upon the earth. And as Isaiah said earlier, "Unless the Lord of hosts had left us a seed, we would have been as Sodom, and been made like Gomorrah."[116]

Remind them of these things, charging them before the Lord not to strive about words to no profit, words that only subvert the hearers. Study to show yourself approved before God, a workman who does not need to be ashamed, one who rightly divides the word of truth. And shun profane and vain chatter, which only increases to more ungodliness. And such words will eat the way a canker does——Hymenaeus and Philetus are examples. These men have erred concerning the truth, saying that the resurrection is already past, and they capsize the faith of some. Nevertheless the foundation of God stands sure, and has this seal——"The Lord knows those who are His." And also this, "Let everyone who names the name of Christ depart from iniquity."

But in a great house there are not just vessels of gold and of silver, but also of wood and of earth——some for honor, and some for dishonor. Therefore if a man purge himself from these doctrines, he will be a vessel for honor, sanctified, and suitable for the master's use, prepared for any good work.[117]

Blessed be the God and Father of our Lord Jesus Christ, who has blessed us with every spiritual blessing in the heavenly places in Christ. According to this, He has chosen us in Him before the foundation of the world, so that we should be holy and without blame before Him in love. He did this having predestined us to our adoption as children by Jesus Christ to Himself, according to the good pleasure of His will, to the praise of His glorious grace, in which He has made us accepted in the beloved. In Him we have redemption through His blood, the forgiveness of sins, according to the riches of His grace, which He made to abound toward us in all wisdom and prudence. This was done having made known to us the mystery of His will, according to His good pleasure which He intended in Himself, as a plan for the fullness of times, so that He might gather all things in Christ together in one, both things in heaven, and also on earth——even in Him. In Him we also have obtained an inheritance, being predestined according to the purpose of Him who works all things according to the counsel of His own will, that we should be to the praise of His glory, we who first trusted in Christ. In Him you also trusted after you heard the word of truth, the gospel of your salvation. And in Him, after you believed, you were sealed with the Holy Spirit of promise, which is the earnest payment of our inheritance, until the redemption of the purchased possession, for the praise of His glory.[118]

What then shall we say? We are saying that the Gentiles, who were not pursuing righteousness, have nevertheless attained to righteousness, meaning the righteousness which is by faith. But Israel, which pursued the law of righteousness, has not attained to that law of righteousness. Why is this? The reason is that they did not seek it *by faith*, but rather by works of the law. For they stumbled over the stumbling stone. As it is written, "Behold, I lay in Zion a stumbling stone and a rock of offense, and whoever believes on Him shall not be ashamed."[119]

THE VEIL OF MOSES

B rothers, my heart's desire and prayer for Israel to God is that they might be saved. For I testify that they have a zeal for God, but not according to knowledge. For they, being ignorant of God's righteousness, and going about to establish their own righteousness, have not submitted themselves to the righteousness of God. For Christ is the whole point of the law——for righteousness to everyone who believes. For Moses describes the righteousness which is "of the law" saying, "that the man who does those things shall live by them." But the righteousness which is by faith speaks in this way, "Do not say in your heart, 'Who shall ascend into heaven?'"——that is, to bring Christ down from above——or, "Who shall descend into the deep?"——that is, to bring up Christ again from the dead. But what does it say? "The word is near you, even in your mouth, and in your heart." That refers to the word of faith, which we preach. We preach that if you confess with your mouth that Jesus is Lord, and if you believe in your heart that God raised Him from the dead, you will be saved. For with the heart man believes unto righteousness, and with the mouth confession is made unto salvation. For the Scripture says, "Whoever believes on Him shall not be ashamed."

Are we beginning again to recommend ourselves? Or do we need, as others do, letters of recommendation for you, or letters of recommendation from you? *You* are our epistle, written on our hearts, known and read by all men——inasmuch as you are manifestly declared to be the epistle of Christ ministered by us, written not with ink, but with the Spirit of the living God, not on tablets of stone, but on the fleshy tablets of the heart. And this is the trust we have through Christ toward God. We do not think ourselves sufficient in ourselves to think anything as from ourselves——our sufficiency is of God. He has made us capable ministers of the new covenant, not of the letter, but of the spirit, for the letter kills, but the spirit gives life.

Now if the ministry of death, written and engraved on stones, was glorious, so that the children of Israel could not steadfastly look at the face of Moses because of the glory of his countenance, a glory that was to be done away, how will the ministry of the Spirit be even more glorious? For if the ministry of condemnation is glory, how much more will the ministry of righteousness excel in glory? For even that which was made glorious like this had no glory in this respect, by reason of the glory that excelled it. For if that which was done away was glorious, how much more glorious is that which remains? Seeing then that we have such hope, we use great plainness of speech.

Not like Moses, who put a veil over his face, so that the children of Israel could not steadfastly look to the fading of that which was to be abolished. But their minds were blinded, for down to this day that same veil remains—— it is not taken away in the reading of the old covenant. Rather, the veil is done away in Christ. Even to this day, whenever Moses is read, the veil remains upon their heart. Nevertheless when it is turned to face the Lord, the veil is taken away. Now the Lord is that Spirit; and where the Spirit of the Lord is, there is liberty. But we all, with open face beholding as in a mirror the glory of the Lord, are changed into the same image from glory to glory, even as by the Spirit of the Lord.[120]

Now there is no difference between the Jew and the Greek, for the same Lord over all is rich unto all who call upon Him. For whoever calls on the name of the Lord shall be saved. But how then will they call on Him in whom they have not believed? And how shall they believe in Him whom they have not heard? And how shall they hear without a preacher? And how shall they preach, unless they are sent?

As it is written, "How beautiful are the feet of those who preach the gospel of peace, and bring glad tidings of good things!" But not all of them have obeyed the gospel. For Isaiah has said, "Lord, who has believed our report?" So then faith comes by hearing, and hearing by the Word of God. But I ask, have they not heard? Yes indeed. "Their voice went out into all the earth, and their words to the ends of the world." But I ask, did Israel not know? First Moses says, "I will provoke you to jealousy by those who are not a people, and by a foolish nation I will anger you." But Isaiah was very bold, and said, "I was found by those who did not seek me. I was revealed to those who did not ask after me." But to Israel He said, "All day long I have put forth my hands to a disobedient and stubborn people."

SPIRIT OF SLUMBER

So I ask then, has God cast away His people? God forbid it. For I am also an Israelite, of the seed of Abraham, of the tribe of Benjamin. God has not cast away His people whom He foreknew. Do you not know what Scripture says of Elijah? Remember how he made intercession to God against Israel, saying, "Lord, they have killed your prophets, and thrown down your altars; I am the only one left, and they are seeking my life." So what does God answer him? "I have reserved to myself seven thousand men, who have not bowed the knee to the image of Baal." In the same way, at this present time also, there is a remnant according to the election of grace. And if by grace, then it cannot be by works——otherwise grace is no longer grace. But if it be by works, then it is no longer grace——otherwise work is no longer work.

What then? Israel has not obtained that which he sought, but the elect have obtained it, and the rest were blinded. This was according to what was written, "God hath given them the spirit of slumber, eyes that they should not see, and ears that they should not hear," down to this day. And David said, "Let their table be made a snare, and a trap, and a stumbling block, and a recompense to them. Let their eyes be darkened, that they may not see, and bend down their back always."

I ask then, have they stumbled that they should fall beyond recovery? God forbid it. But rather salvation has come to the Gentiles through their fall, in order to provoke Israel to jealousy. Now if their fall is the riches of the world, and their diminution the riches of the Gentiles, what will their fullness come to? For I am speaking to you Gentiles——in that I am the apostle of the Gentiles, I magnify my office. I do this so that if by any means I might provoke my kinsmen to jealousy, and so might save some of them.[121]

Tell me, you who desire to be under the law, do you not hear the law? For it is written that Abraham had two sons, one by a slave woman, the other by a free woman. But he who was born of the slave woman was born according to the flesh, while he who was born of the free woman was of the promise. These things are an allegory——for these women are two covenants. One is from Mount Sinai, which bears slave children, which is Hagar. For this Hagar is Mount Sinai in Arabia, and answers to the Jerusalem which now is, and is in slavery together with her children.

But the Jerusalem which is above is free, who is the mother of us all. For it is written, "Rejoice, you barren one who bears no children; break forth and cry, you who do not travail, for the desolate woman now has many more children than she who has a husband."

Now we, brothers, are the children of promise just as Isaac was. But back then, the one born according to the flesh persecuted the one born according to the Spirit, and it is the same way now. And so what does the Scripture say? "Cast out the slave woman and her son, for the son of the slave woman shall not be heir with the son of the free woman." So then, brothers, we are not children of the slave woman, but of the free.[122]

For you, brothers, became followers of the churches of God in Judaea which are in Christ Jesus. For you also suffered similar things from your own countrymen, even as they have from the Jews. For they both killed the Lord Jesus, *and* their own prophets, and have persecuted us. They do not please God, and are contrary to all men. They prohibit us from speaking to the Gentiles that they might be saved, to fill up their sins completely. For wrath is come upon them to the uttermost.[123]

Finally, my brothers, rejoice in the Lord. To write the same things to you is not a grief to me, and it is safe for you. Beware of dogs, beware of evil workers, beware of the mutilators. For we are the true circumcision, who worship God in the spirit, and rejoice in Christ Jesus, and have *no* confidence in the flesh.

Though if anybody could have confidence in the flesh, I certainly could. If any other man thinks he has grounds to trust in the flesh, I far more. I was circumcised on the eighth day, of the stock of Israel, of the tribe of Benjamin, a Hebrew of Hebrews. As touching the law, I was a Pharisee; as concerning zeal, I persecuted the church; as touching the righteousness which is in the law, I was blameless. But whatever things were profit to me, those I counted a complete loss for Christ. Yes and doubt-less, I count all things as a loss compared to the excellence of the knowledge of Christ Jesus my Lord. He is the One for whom I have suffered the loss of all things, and reckon them all as so much sewage, that I may win Christ.[124]

I wish to God you could bear with me a little in my folly, and indeed really bear with me. For I am jealous for you with a godly jealousy——for I have betrothed you to one husband, in order that I might present you as a chaste virgin to Christ. But I fear, by some means, as the serpent deceived Eve through his subtlety, so also your minds should be corrupted from the simplicity that is found in Christ. For if some fellow comes and preaches another Jesus, whom we have not preached, or if you receive another spirit, which you did not receive, or an-other gospel, which you have not accepted, you put up with *him* well enough.

Now I suppose I was not a whisker behind the most preeminent apostles. Though I am rude in speech, yet not in *knowledge* . . . oh, but what we are has been thoroughly made manifest among you in everything. Have I offended by abasing myself so that you might be exalted, in that I preached to you the gospel of God without charge? I robbed other churches, taking wages from them, in order to do you service. And when I was present with you, and lacked, I burdened not one of you. For that which I need-ed the brothers from Macedonia supplied. In all things I have kept myself from being a burden to you, and am going to keep it that way. As the truth of Christ is in me, no man shall stop me from boasting this way throughout the regions of Achaia. Why is this? Because I don't love you? *God* knows. But what I am doing I will continue to do, so that I may cut off opportunities from those who desire opportunities against us. This is so that *whatever* they glory in, they might be found in the same position we are in. For these men are false apostles, deceitful workers, who transform themselves into the apostles of Christ. And this is no marvel, for Satan himself is transformed into an angel of light. It is therefore no great thing if his ministers are also transformed into ministers of righteousness——whose end shall be according to their works.

I will say it again. Let no man think me a fool. But if you do, then receive me as a fool so that I might boast in myself a little. What I am about to say is not according to the Lord, but as it were foolishly, in a bit of confident boasting. Seeing that many glory according to the flesh, I will glory in the same way also. For you allow for fools gladly, seeing that you yourselves are so wise. For you allow it, if a man brings you into slavery, if a man devours you, if a man robs you, if a man exalts himself above you, if a man strikes you in the face.

Concerning reproach, I speak as though we were weak. Nevertheless, if any are bold——I speak as a fool——I am bold also. Are they Hebrews? So am I. Are they Israelites? So am I. Are they the seed of Abraham? So am I. Are they ministers of Christ? Remember I speak as a fool——I am more. I was in labors more abundantly, in stripes above counting, in prison more frequently, in deathly perils often. Five times the Jews administered 39 stripes. Three times I was beaten with rods, and once was I stoned. Three times I suffered shipwreck, and for a night and a day I have been adrift at sea. I journeyed often, and was in perils by water, in perils by robbers, in perils by my own countrymen, in perils by the heathen, in perils in the city, in perils in the wilderness, in perils in the sea, and in perils among false brothers. I was in weariness and painfulness, in frequent watches, in hunger and thirst, in common fasting, in cold and nakedness. Beside all these things from outside, there was that which came upon me daily, which was the care of all the churches.

Who is weak, and I am not weak with them? Who is stumbled with me burning? So if I have to glory, I will glory in the things which deal with my infirmities. The God and Father of our Lord Jesus Christ, who is blessed forever, knows that I am not lying. There was one other thing. In Damascus under King Aretas, the governor sealed up the city of the Damascenes with a garrison, wanting to apprehend me. I was let down through a window in the wall by a basket, and escaped from him that way.[125]

ONE OLIVE TREE

Now if the casting away of the Jews is the reconciling of the world, what will the receiving of them be, but life from the dead? For if the first fruits are holy, the lump is holy also, and if the root is holy, so are the branches.

So if some of the branches were broken off, and you, being a wild olive tree, were grafted in among them, and with them you partook of the root and fatness of the olive tree, make sure of this. Do not boast against the branches. But if you boast, recall you do not bear the root, but the root bears you. Now one of you might say that branches were broken off that you might be grafted in. Very well. They were broken off because of unbelief, and you stand by faith. Do not be high minded, but rather fear. For if God did not spare the natural branches, take heed lest He not do the same to you. Consider therefore the kindness and severity of God——on those who fell, severity, but toward you, kindness, if you continue in His kindness. Otherwise you also will be cut off.

And they also, if they do not remain in unbelief, shall be grafted back in again, for God is able to graft them in again. For if you were cut out of the olive tree which is wild by nature, and contrary to nature were grafted into a good olive tree, how much more shall these, the natural branches, be grafted back into their own olive tree?

For I would not have you be ignorant of this mystery, brothers, lest you become wise in your own conceits. A partial blindness has happened to Israel, until the fullness of the Gentiles has come in. And so all Israel will be saved, as it is written, "A Deliverer shall come out of Zion, and He will turn ungodliness away from Jacob. For this is my covenant for them, when I will take away their sins."

So concerning the gospel, they are enemies for your sakes, but as touching the election, they are beloved for their fathers' sakes. For the gifts and calling of God are irrevocable. Just as in time past you did not obey God, but have now obtained mercy through their disobedience, even so now they do not obey, so that through your mercy they also may obtain mercy. For God has consigned *everyone* to disobedience so that He might have mercy upon all.[126]

Men of Israel, and you who fear God, give me a hearing. The God of this nation (the people of Israel) chose our fathers, and exalted the people when they were dwelling as strangers in the land of Egypt. With a high arm He brought them out of it. For about forty years He tolerated behavior in the wilderness.

And when He had destroyed seven nations in the land of Canaan, by lot He divided their land for them. And after that He gave judges to them for about four hundred and fifty years, until the time of Samuel the prophet. And after that they desired a king, so God gave Saul the son of Kish to them, a man from the tribe of Benjamin, and he ruled for forty years. And when He had removed him, He raised up David for them to be their king, concerning whom He also testified and said, "I have found David the son of Jesse, a man after my own heart, who shall fulfill all my will." From this man's seed God has, according to His promise, raised up for Israel a Savior, Jesus. Before His coming John had preached the baptism of repentance to all the people of Israel. And as John filled out his course, he said, "Who do you think I am? I am not He. But, behold, one comes after me, and the shoes of His feet I am not worthy to unloose."

Men and brothers, children of the line of Abraham, and whoever among you fears God, to *you* is this word of salvation sent. For those who dwell in Jerusalem, and their rulers, did not recognize Him. Neither did they hear the voices of the prophets which are read every sabbath day, but they have fulfilled the prophets in condemning Him. And though they found nothing worth of death in Him, nevertheless they sought for Pilate to slay Him. And when they had fulfilled everything that was written about Him, they took Him down from the tree, and laid Him in a sepulcher.

But God raised Him from the dead. He seen for many days by those who came up with Him to Jerusalem from Galilee, and they are His witnesses to the people. And we declare glad tidings to you, how the promise that was made to the fathers has been fulfilled by God for us their children. It was fulfilled in that He has raised up Jesus again, as it is also written in the second psalm, "You are my Son, this day I have begotten you."

And concerning the fact that He raised Him up from the dead, never again to return to corruption, He said, "I will give you the sure mercies of David." And therefore He says in another psalm, "You will not allow your Holy One to see corruption." For David, after he had served his own generation by the will of God, fell asleep, and was laid to rest with his fathers, and he saw corruption. But He whom God raised up again saw no corruption.

Therefore, let it be it known to you, men and brothers, that forgiveness of sins is preached to you through this man. By Him any who believe are justified from all things from which you could not be justified from under the law of Moses. Take care then, lest what is spoken of by the prophets comes upon you. "Behold, you despisers, and wonder and perish. For I do a work in your days, a work which you will in no way believe, even if a man declares it to you."[127]

So then, brothers, I would not have you be ignorant of the fact that all our fathers were under the cloud, and all passed through the sea. They were all baptized into Moses in the cloud and in the sea, and they all ate the same spiritual food, and drank the same spiritual drink. For they drank from that spiritual Rock that followed them, and that Rock was Christ.

But God was not well pleased with many of them, for they were overthrown in the wilderness. Now these things were examples for us, with the intent we should not lust after evil things, the same way they also lusted. Neither should you be idolaters, as some of them were, as it is written, "The people sat down to eat and drink, and rose up to play." And neither let us commit fornication, as some of them did, and 23,000 of them fell in one day. Neither let us tempt Christ, as some of them did, and were destroyed by serpents. Neither should you murmur, as some of them also murmured, and were destroyed of the destroyer.

Now all these things happened to them as examples, and they are written down for our admonition, upon whom the ends of the ages have come. Therefore let the one who thinks he stands take heed lest he fall. There is no temptation that has taken you except what is common to man—but God is faithful, who will not allow you to be tempted beyond what you are able. But with the temptation He will also make a way of escape, so that you will be able to stand it. Therefore, my dearly beloved, flee from idolatry. I speak as to wise men—you judge what I say.[128]

A CUP OF BLESSING

The cup of blessing which we bless, is it not the communion of the blood of Christ? The bread which we break, is it not the communion of the body of Christ? For we, being many, are one loaf and one body, for we are all partakers of that one loaf. Consider Israel according the flesh. Do not those who eat the sacrifices have communion in the altar?

What am I saying then? That an idol is anything, or that which is offered in sacrifice to idols is anything? What I am saying is that the things which the Gentiles sacrifice, they sacrifice to devils, and not to God. And I do not want you to have communion with devils. You cannot drink the cup of the Lord and also the cup of devils. You cannot partake in the Lord's table, and *also* in the table of devils. Do we want to provoke the Lord to jealousy? Are we stronger than He is?[129]

O you Corinthians, we have spoken to you freely, our heart is wide open to you. You are not shut out by us, but have been shut out by your own affections. Now in return——I speak as to my own children——open your hearts wide also.

Do not be unequally yoked together with unbelievers. For what fellowship does righteousness have with unrighteousness? And what communion does light have with darkness? And what sort of concord is there between Christ and Belial? Or what portion does a believer have with an infidel? And what agreement does the temple of God have with idols?

For you are the temple of the living God. As God has said, "I will dwell in them, and walk with them; I will be their God, and they will be my people. Therefore come out from among them, and be separate, says the Lord. Do not touch the unclean thing, and I will receive you. And I will be a Father to you, and you shall be my sons and daughters, says the Lord Almighty."[130]

Therefore remember that in time past you were Gentiles according to the flesh. You were called the Uncircumcision by those who were called the Circumcision——circumcision according to the flesh, the kind done with hands. At that time you were without Christ, and were aliens from the commonwealth of Israel, strangers from the covenants of promise, with no hope, and without God in the world. But now in Christ Jesus you who were at one time far off have been brought near by the blood of Christ.

For He is our peace, who has made both Jew and Gentile one, and has broken down the middle wall of partition between us. He did this having abolished the enmity in His flesh, meaning the law of commandments contained within the ordinances, in order to make one new man out of the two in Himself, thus making peace, that He might reconcile both to God in one body by means of the cross, slaying their enmity that way. And He came and preached peace to you who were far off, and to those who were near. For through Him we both have access by one Spirit to the Father.

Now therefore you are no longer strangers and foreigners, but fellow citizens together with the saints, and in the household of God. And you are built upon the foundation of the apostles and prophets, with Jesus Christ Himself as the chief cornerstone——in whom the entire building is tightly framed together, and grows into a holy temple in the Lord. In Him you are built together as a habitation of God through the Spirit.

So for this cause I, Paul, a prisoner of Jesus Christ for you Gentiles . . . if you have heard of the administration of the grace of God which was given me for all of you. I mean how by revelation He made known to me the mystery——as I wrote briefly before——by which when you read, you might understand my knowledge into the mystery of Christ. In other ages, this was not made known to the sons of men, as it has now been revealed to His holy apostles and prophets by the Spirit. I mean that the Gentiles should be fellow heirs with the Jews, and in the same body, and partakers of His promise in Christ by the gospel. Of this truth I was made a minister, according to the gift of the grace of God given to me by the effectual working of His power. This grace was given to me, who is less than the least of all saints, that I should preach among the Gentiles the unsearchable riches of Christ, in order to make all men see what is the fellowship of this mystery, which from the beginning of the world has been hidden in God, who created all things by Jesus Christ. He did this with the intent that now the manifold wisdom of God might be displayed by the church to the principalities and powers in the heavenly places. All this was according to the eternal purpose which He intended in Christ Jesus our Lord. In Him we have boldness and access with confidence by His faith. This is why I desire that you do not faint at my tribulations for you——they are your glory.[131]

I therefore, the prisoner of the Lord, plead with you to walk worthy of the calling with which you are called, with all humility and meekness, with patience, bearing with one another in love. Do this while endeavouring to keep the unity of the Spirit in the bond of peace.

There is one body, and one Spirit, even as you are called in one hope of your calling——one Lord, one faith, one baptism, one God and Father of all, who is above all, and through all, and in you all. But to each one of us is given grace according to the measure of the gift of Christ. Therefore He says, "When He ascended up on high, He led captivity captive, and gave gifts unto men." Now when it says He ascended, what does it assume but that He also first descended into the lower parts of the earth? He who descended is the same one also who ascended far above all the heavens, so that He might fill all things.

And He gave some to be apostles; and some, prophets; and some, evangelists; and some others, pastors and teachers——for the completion of the saints, for the work of the ministry, for the edifying of the body of Christ. This is so we would all come to the unity of the faith, and of the knowledge of the Son of God, up to a perfect man, unto the measure of the stature of the fullness of Christ. Then we will no longer be children, tossed this way and that, carried about by every wind of doctrine, by the sleight of men, and their cunning craftiness, which they use to deceive as they lie in wait. But rather, speaking the truth in love, we will grow up into Him in all things, even into the head, who is Christ. He is the one from whom the whole body is joined and held together by what every joint supplies, and as every part works effectively as it should, makes the body grow as it builds itself up in love.[132]

RESURRECTION

Now if Christ is preached as risen from the dead, how do some say among you that there is no resurrection of the dead? If there is no resurrection of the dead, then Christ was not raised. And if Christ is not risen, then our preaching is vain, and your faith is vain as well. In addition to that, we are revealed as false witnesses concerning God— because we have testified that God raised up Christ, whom He did not raise if the dead are not raised.

If the dead do not rise, then Christ did not rise. And if Christ was not raised, your faith is vanity and you are still in your sins. And also those who have fallen asleep in Christ have simply perished. If we only have hope in Christ in *this* life, we are the most miserable of men.

But in fact Christ is risen from the dead, and has become the first fruits of those who slept. For since death came by man, so also the resurrection of the dead came by man. For as in Adam all die, even so in Christ shall all be made alive. But each man in his own order—Christ the first fruits, and then afterward those who belong to Christ at His coming.

Then comes the end, when He will have delivered up the kingdom to God, even the Father, after He has put down all rule and authority and power. For He must reign until He has put all enemies under His feet. The last enemy to be destroyed will be death. For He has put *all* things under His feet.

But when He says "all things are put under Him," it is obvious that He Himself is excepted who put all things under Him. And when all things are subdued under Him, then the Son Himself will be subject to the One who put all things under Him, so that God may be all in all.

If the dead are not raised at all, what will those people do who practice baptism for the dead? Why would *they* baptize for the dead?

And why would we stand in jeopardy every hour? I protest——by my pride in you, which I have in Christ Jesus our Lord——I die every day. Humanly speaking, what did I gain by fighting with wild beasts at Ephesus? If the dead do not rise, let us eat and drink, for tomorrow we die. Do not be deceived——evil companions corrupt good morals. Wake up to righteousness, and do not sin. For some do not have the knowledge of God——I speak this to your shame.[133]

But we have this treasure in earthen vessels, so that the excellence of the power may be of God, and not of us. We are troubled on every side, but not distressed. We are perplexed, but not in despair. We are persecuted, but not forsaken, cast down, but not destroyed. We always carry about in the body the dying of the Lord Jesus, so that the life of Jesus might be made manifest in our body. For we who are alive are always delivered to death for Jesus' sake, so that the life also of Jesus might be made manifest in our mortal flesh. So then death works in us, but life in you.

We have the same spirit of faith, as it is written, "I believed, and therefore I have spoken." We also believe, and therefore we speak, knowing that He who raised up the Lord Jesus shall raise up us also by Jesus, and shall present us together with you. For all things are for your sakes, so that abundant grace might——through the thanksgiving of many——redound to the glory of God. For this reason we do not faint. Though our outer man perish, yet the inner man is renewed day after day. For our light affliction, which is just for a moment, works for us a far more exceeding and eternal weight of glory. We do not look at the things which are seen, but rather at the things which are not seen. For the things which are seen are temporal, but the things which are not seen are eternal.[134]

But some man will come and say, "How are the dead raised up? What kind of body do they have?" You fool, that which you sow in the ground is not made alive unless it first dies. And when you sow, you do not sow the body that *will* be, but just grain——perhaps wheat or some other kind of grain. But God gives it a body as it has pleased Him, and to each seed its own body.

All flesh is not the same flesh. There is one kind of flesh with men, another flesh for beasts, another for fish, and another for birds. There are also celestial bodies and terrestrial bodies——but the glory of the celestial is one, and the glory of the terrestrial is another. There is one glory of the sun, and another glory of the moon, and yet another glory of the stars. One star differs from another star in glory.

It is the same way with the resurrection of the dead. The body is sown in corruption; it is raised imperishable. It is sown in dishonor; it is raised in glory. It is sown in weakness; it is raised in power. It is sown a natural body; it is raised a spiritual body——there *is* a natural body and a spiritual body. And so it is written, "The first man Adam was made a living soul." The last Adam was made a life-giving spirit. But it was not the spiritual that was first, but rather that which is natural——the spiritual came afterward. The first man was of the earth, and *earthy*; the second man is the Lord from heaven. As is the earthy, so also are those who are of the earth. And as is the heavenly, so also are those who are heavenly. And as we have once borne the image of the earthy, so also we shall bear the image of the heavenly.

Now brothers, I say this——flesh and blood cannot inherit the kingdom of God. Neither can corruption inherit the imperishable. Look at this——I will show you a mystery. We will not all sleep, but we will all be changed. In a moment, in the twinkling of an eye, at the last trumpet—— for the trumpet will sound, and the dead will be raised incorruptible, and we will be changed. For this perishable body must put on the imperishable, and this mortal body must put on immortality. So when this perishable body will have put on the imperishable, and this mortal body will have put on immortality, then that saying shall come to pass as it is written, "Death is swallowed up in victory. O death, where is your sting? O grave, where is your victory?" The sting of death is sin, and the strength of sin is in the law.

But thanks be given to God, who gives us the victory through our Lord Jesus Christ. Therefore, my beloved brothers, you be steadfast, immoveable, and always abounding in the work of the Lord. For you know that in the Lord your labor is not in vain.[135]

UNITY OF MIND

Now I plead with you, brothers, in the name of our Lord Jesus Christ, that you all speak the same thing, and that there be no divisions among you; but that you be joined together perfectly in the same mind and in the same judgment. For it has been declared to me of you, my brothers, by those who are of the house of Chloe, that there are contentions among you.

Now this I say, that every one of you says things like, "I am of Paul," "I of Apollos," "I of Cephas," and "*I of Christ.*" Is Christ divided? Was Paul crucified for you? Or were you baptized in the name of Paul? I thank God I baptized none of you except for Crispus and Gaius-- lest any should say that I had baptized anyone in my own name. And yes, I also baptized the household of Stephanas. Besides that I do not know whether I baptized anyone else.[136]

O the depth of the riches of both the wisdom and knowledge of God! How unsearchable are His judgments, and His ways past finding out! For who has known the mind of the Lord? Or who has been His counselor? Or who has first given to Him, that he should be repaid again? For of Him, and through Him, and to Him, are all things——to whom be glory forever. Amen.[137]

Now in this I have to declare to you that I cannot praise you. When you come together it is not for the better, but for the worse. First of all, when you come together in the church, I hear that there are divisions among you, and I partly believe it. For there must be factions among you, so that those who are genuine may be revealed among you. When you gather together in one place, it is not to eat the Lord's Supper. For in eating one takes his food, another is hungry, and another one is drunken. *What?* Do you not have houses to eat and to drink in? Or do you despise the church of God, shaming those who have nothing? What shall I say to you? Shall I praise you in this? I will not praise you.

For I have received from the Lord that which I also delivered to you. On the same night He was betrayed, the Lord Jesus took bread, and when He had given thanks, He broke it, and said, "Take, eat. This is my body, which is broken for you. Do this in remembrance of me." And in the same manner, when He had eaten, He also took the cup, saying, "This cup is the new covenant in my blood. This do, as often as you drink it, in remembrance of Me." For as often as you eat this bread and drink this cup, you show forth the Lord's death until He comes. Therefore whoever eats this bread and drinks this cup of the Lord unworthily shall be guilty of the body and blood of the Lord. So let a man examine himself, and then let him eat of that bread, and drink of that cup. For he who eats and drinks unworthily, eats and drinks condemnation to himself, not discerning the Lord's body. For this reason many are weak and sickly among you, and many even sleep.

For if we would judge ourselves, we would not *be* judged. But when we are judged, we are being chastened by the Lord so that we should not be condemned with the world. Therefore, my brothers, when you come together to eat, wait for one another. And if a man is hungry, let him eat at home——so that when you come together it is not for condemnation. The other issues I will set in order when I come.[138]

If there is therefore any consolation in Christ, any comfort of love, any fellowship of the Spirit, any tender mercies, then fulfil my joy by being likeminded, having the same love, being of one accord, and of one mind. Do nothing through strife or vainglory, but in humility of mind let each one esteem the other ahead of himself. Each man should not look after his own things, but each man also look after the things of others.

Let this mind be in you, which was also in Christ Jesus. He, being in the form of God, did not think equality with God a thing to be seized. Rather, He made Himself of no reputation, and took upon Himself the form of a slave, and was made in the likeness of men.

And being found in the form of a man, He humbled Himself, and became obedient unto death, even the death on the cross. Therefore God also has highly exalted Him, and given Him a name which is above every name——that at the name of Jesus every knee should bow, whether things in heaven, or things on earth, and things under the earth. And that every tongue should confess that Jesus Christ is Lord, to the glory of God the Father.[139]

GIFTS AND SERVICE

I therefore plead with you, brothers, by the mercies of God, to present your bodies a living sacrifice, holy and acceptable to God, which is your reasonable worship. And do not be conformed to this world, but rather be transformed by the renewing of your mind, so that you may prove what is the good, acceptable, and perfect will of God.

For I say to every man among you, through the grace given to me, not to think of himself more highly than he ought to think. But rather he should think soberly, according to how God has apportioned to each man a measure of faith. For we have many members in one body, and not all members have the same office. So we, being many, are one body in Christ, and all of us are members one of another. Having then gifts that differ according to the grace given to us——if prophecy, let us prophesy according to our proportion of faith; if serving, in our service; if teaching, in our teaching; if exhorting, in exhortation: if generosity, let him give with sincerity; if governance, with diligence; if showing mercy, then with cheerfulness.[140]

So concerning spiritual gifts, brothers, I would not have you ignorant. You know that you were pagans, carried away to these mute idols, even as you were led. Therefore I want you to understand that no man speaking by the Spirit of God can call Jesus accursed, and that no man can say that Jesus is Lord, except by the Holy Spirit.

Now there are diverse gifts, but the same Spirit. And there are differences of service, but the same Lord. And there are varieties of work, but it is the same God who works all in all. But to each man the Spirit is manifested for the common good. For one man by the Spirit has the word of wisdom; to another the word of knowledge by the same Spirit; to another faith by the same Spirit; to another the gifts of healing by the same Spirit; to another the working of miracles; to another prophecy; to another discerning of spirits; to another various kinds of tongues; to another the interpretation of these tongues. All these are done by that same Spirit, apportioning to each man individually as He wills.

For as the body is one, and has many members, and all the members of that one body, being many, are still one body, so also it is with Christ. For by one Spirit we are all baptized into one body, whether we are Jews or Gentiles, whether we are slave or free, and we have all been made to drink of one Spirit. For the body is not just one member, but many. If the foot were to say, "Because I am not the hand, I am not in the body," is it therefore not in the body? And if the ear were to say, "Because I am not the eye, I am not in the body," is it therefore not in the body? If the whole body were an eye, where would the hearing be? If the whole were the ear, where would the smelling be?

But now God has set the members, each one of them, in the body, as it has pleased Him. If they were all one member, where would the body be? But as it is, they are many members, and yet one body. And the eye cannot say to the hand, "I have no need of you," nor again the head to the feet, "I have no need of you."

No, all members of the body are necessary, even those which seem to be weak. And those members of the body which we think of as less honorable, upon these we bestow more abundant honor; and our private members are granted a greater modesty. For our presentable parts have no such need, but God has composed the body in such a way as that more abundant honor was given to those parts which lacked it. This is so that there would be no division in the body; but that all the members would show the same kind of care for one another. And so when one member suffers, all the members suffer with it. And when one member is honored, all the members rejoice with it. So then you are the body of Christ together, and individual members in particular.

God has set some up in the church this way: first apostles, second prophets, third teachers, and then after that miracles, then gifts of healings, helps, administration, various tongues. Are all apostles? Are all prophets? Are all teachers? Are all workers of miracles? Do all have all gifts of healing? Do all speak with tongues? Do all interpret? Obviously not. But earnestly desire the best gifts, and I will show you an even better more excellent way.[141]

Now we plead with you, brothers, to know those who labor among you, and are over you in the Lord, and admonish you. Make sure to esteem them very highly in love for their work's sake. And be at peace among yourselves.[142]

Godliness with contentment is great gain. For we brought nothing into this world, and it is most certain we can carry nothing out. So having food and clothing, let us be content with that. Those who would be rich fall into temptations and snares, and into many foolish and harmful lusts, which drown men in destruction and ruin. For the love of money is the root of all kinds of evil, which, when some coveted, caused them to wander from the faith, and they have pierced themselves through with many sorrows. But you, O man of God, flee from these things. Follow after righteousness, godliness, faith, love, patience, meekness.[143]

This is a true saying. If a man desire the office of an overseer, he desires a good work. An overseer then must be blameless, the husband of one wife, vigilant, sober, of good behavior, given to hospitality, and able to teach. He should not be given to wine, no bully, not greedy for dirty money, but rather patient, not a brawler, and not covetous. He should be one who rules his own household well, having his children in obedience with all dignity. For if a man does not know how to manage his own household, how will he be able to take care of the church of God? He should not be a young scholar, lest being lifted up with pride he fall into the condemnation of the devil. In addition, he must have a good report among those who are outside, lest he fall into the reproach and snare of the devil.

For this reason I left you in Crete, that you should set in order the things that were lacking, and ordain elders in every city, as I had appointed to you. I wanted such elders to be blameless, the husband of one wife, having faithful children not accused of riot or unruly. For an overseer must be blameless, as the steward of God; not self-willed, not quick-tempered, not given to wine, no striker, not given to dirty money. Rather, he should be a lover of hospitality, a lover of good men, sober, just, holy, and temperate. He should hold fast the faithful word as he has been taught, in order that he might be able by sound doctrine both to exhort and to convince those who contradict him.[144]

Let the elders who rule well be counted worthy of double honor, especially those who labor in the word and doctrine. For Scripture says, "You shall not muzzle the ox that treads out the grain," and, "The laborer is worthy of his hire." Do not receive an accusation against an elder unless you have two or three witnesses. Those who sin, rebuke in front of them all, so that others may stand in fear. And I charge you before God, and the Lord Jesus Christ, and the elect angels, that you observe these things without giving preference to one over another, doing nothing by partiality. Lay hands suddenly on no man, neither be partaker of other men's sins. Keep yourself pure.[145]

In the same way, the deacons should be dignified, not double-tongued, not given to much wine, not greedy for dirty money. They should hold the mystery of the faith with a pure conscience. And they should first be tested, and then let them assume the office of a deacon, having been found blameless.

And also, the women must carry themselves with dignity. They must not slander, they should be sober, and faithful in all things.

Let the deacons be the husbands of one wife, ruling their children and their own households well. For they that have used the office of a deacon well obtain for themselves a good standing, and great confidence in the faith which is in Christ Jesus.[146]

Now I, brothers, could not speak to you as to spiritual men, but rather as to carnal, even as to babes in Christ. I have fed you with milk, and not with solid food. For up to this point you were not able to take it, neither are you able now. For you are still carnal——why else would there be among you envying, and strife, and divisions. Are you not carnal, and walk as mere men?

For when one says, "I am of Paul," and another, "I am of Apollos," are you not carnal? Who then is Paul, and who is Apollos, but ministers by whom you believed, even as the Lord apportioned to every man? I have planted, and Apollos watered; but God is the One who gives the increase. So the man who plants is nothing, and neither is the one who waters, but rather God who gives the increase.

Now he who plants and he who waters are one, and every man will receive his own reward according to his own labor. For we are laborers together with God, and you are God's planted field, you are God's building.

MASTER BUILDER

According to the grace of God which was given to me, as a wise master builder, I have laid the foundation, and another man builds on it. But let every man take note how he builds upon it. For no other foundation can a man lay than what has been laid, which is Jesus Christ. Now if any man build upon this foundation with gold, silver, precious stones, wood, hay, or stubble, what every man has done in his work will be made manifest. For the day will declare it, because it will be revealed by fire; and the fire shall test the quality of every man's work. If any man's work remains which he has built on the foundation, he shall receive a reward. If any man's work is consumed, he shall suffer the loss, but he himself will be saved, but as it were through fire.

Do you not know that you are the temple of God, and that the Spirit of God dwells in you? If any man defiles the temple of God, God will destroy that man—for the temple of God is holy, which temple you are. Let no man deceive himself. If any man among you seems to be wise in this world, then let him become a fool, so that he may actually be wise. For the wisdom of this world is foolishness to God. For it is written, "He takes the wise in their own craftiness." And again, "The Lord knows the thoughts of the wise, that they are vain." Therefore let no man glory in *men*. For all things are yours——whether Paul, or Apollos, or Cephas, or the world, or life, or death, or things present, or things to come——all things are yours. And you are Christ's, and Christ is God's.[147]

GIFTS AND GRACE

Moreover, brothers, we want you to know of
the grace of God bestowed on the churches
of Macedonia. We want you to know how
in a great trial of affliction, the abundance of their joy
together with their deep poverty resulted in the abundant
riches of their liberality. For they gave what they could, I
can testify, yes, and beyond what they could, of their own
volition. They earnestly pleaded with us for the privilege
of partaking in the relief of the saints. And they did this,
not as we expected, but they gave themselves first to the
Lord, and then to us by the will of God.

Therefore we urged Titus, since he had begun the
work, that he would complete among you this same labor
of grace. So therefore, as you excel in everything——in
faith, and speech, and knowledge, and in all diligence, and
in your love to us——see that you abound in this grace
also. I say this not as a command, but to show by the zeal
of others that your love is sincere. For you know the grace
of our Lord Jesus Christ, that, though He was rich, yet
for your sakes He became poor, so that you through His
poverty might become rich.

Now here is my advice. This is a help to you, who began this work a year ago, not only to do it, but to be eager to do it. Now therefore accomplish the doing of it,

as there was a readiness to do it, so also the performance might match it——out of what you have. For if there is a willing mind, then it is accepted according to what a man has, and not according to what he does not have. For I do not want other men to be eased, and you burdened. Rather that there be an equality, so that at this time your abundance might supply their want, and that their abundance also might supply your want——that there might be equity. As it is written, "He that gathered much had nothing left over; and he that gathered little had no lack."

But thanks be to God, who put the same earnest care that I have for you into the heart of Titus. For indeed he accepted our appeal, but being very eager, of his own accord he went to you. And we have sent the brother with him, a man whose praise is in the gospel throughout all the churches. Not only that, but he was also chosen by the churches to travel with us with this gift, which is administered by us to the glory of the same Lord, and to manifest our good will. We want to take this precaution, that no man should fault us for our ministry of this generous gift. We want to do what is honest and right, not only in the sight of the Lord, but also in the sight of men. And we have sent our brother with them, who has often proved diligent in many ways, but now even more diligent, because of his great confidence in you. As for Titus, he is my partner and fellow worker among you. If any ask about our brothers, they are the messengers of the churches, and the glory of Christ. Therefore, in front of the churches, show them the proof of your love, and vindicate our boasting on your behalf.[148]

So then, as regards the ministry for the saints, it is superfluous for me to write to you. For I know your eagerness of mind, concerning which I boasted of you to those in Macedonia. I said that Achaia was ready a year ago, and your zeal has stirred up many people. Yet I have sent the brothers ahead, lest our boasting of you should be in vain in this regard. As I said, I want you to be ready, lest it happen that men from Macedonia come with me, and find you unprepared. We, not to mention you, would be ashamed of our confident boasting. That is why I thought it necessary to exhort the brothers, so that they would come to you earlier, and gather up your bounty beforehand. If you have prior notice, then the same would be ready, as a matter of generosity, and not as affected by covetousness.

But this I say: He who sows sparingly will also reap sparingly. And he who sows bountifully will also reap bountifully. Let every man give according to how he purposes in his heart——not grudgingly, or of necessity: for God loves a cheerful giver. And God is able to make all grace abound toward you, so that you, always having all sufficiency in everything, may abound in every good work. As it is written, "He has dispersed abroad; he has given to the poor; His righteousness remains forever." Now He that ministers seed to the sower both ministers bread for your food, and multiplies your seed sown, and increases the fruits of your righteousness, being enriched in everything to all abundance, which causes thanksgiving to God because of us. For the administration of this service not only supplies the want of the saints, but is abundant also by many thanksgivings unto God. While in the proof of this ministry they will glorify God for your submission to your confession of the gospel of Christ, and for your liberal generosity to them, and to all men. At the same time, by their prayers for you, they yearn after you because of the exceeding grace of God in you. And thanks be to God for His unspeakable gift![149]

Am I not an apostle? Am I not free? Have I not seen Jesus Christ our Lord? And are you not my work in the Lord? If I am not an apostle to others, yet doubtless I am to you——for *you* are the seal of my apostleship in the Lord. My answer to those who examine me is this——do we not have the right to eat and to drink? Do we not have the right to lead around a sister, a wife, as the other apostles do, as the Lord's brothers do, and as Cephas does? Do not Barnabas and I have the right to forbear working?

Who goes to war on his own accounts? Who plants a vineyard, and does not eat the fruit of it? Or who feeds a flock, and does not partake of the milk of that flock? Do I say this on a human level? Does not the law say the same? For it is written in the law of Moses, "You shall not muzzle the mouth of the ox that treads out the grain." Does God focus on the oxen? Or does He say this for our sake? For our sake, no doubt, this was written. For he who plows should plow in hope, and he who threshes in hope should be partaker of that hope. If we have sown spiritual things among you, is it a great thing if we reap your material things? If others have this claim on you, do we not more? Nevertheless we did not use this claim, but endure all things, lest we should hinder the gospel of Christ.

Do you not know that those who minister in holy things live by the things of the temple? And that those who wait at the altar are partakers of the altar? In the same way, the Lord has ordained that those who preach the gospel should live by the gospel. But I have not used this prerogative——neither have I written this so that this should be done for me. For I would rather die than that any man should make my glorying empty.

For though I preach the gospel, I have nothing to glory in. For necessity is laid upon me——yes, woe to me if I do *not* preach the gospel! For if I do this thing willingly, I have a return. But if against my will, the duty of the gospel remains with me. What is my return then? Truly, it is that when I preach the gospel, I may present that gospel of Christ free of charge, in order that I do not abuse my rights in that gospel. For though I am free from all men, yet at the same time I have made myself slave unto all, that I might gain even more.

So to the Jews I became as a Jew, in order to win the Jews. To those who are under the law, as though under the law, so that I might win those who are under the law. To those who were apart from the law, as apart from the law——although I am not without law before God, but rather am under the law of Christ——in order that I might win those who are apart from the law. To the weak I became as weak, in order that I might win the weak. I am made all things to all men, in order that I might by all means save some. And this I do for the gospel's sake, that I might be partaker of it together with you.[150]

HARD WORDS

Receive us, please. We have wronged no man; we have corrupted no man; we have defrauded no man. I do not speak this to condemn you, for as I have said before, that you are in our hearts so that we might die and live with you. My boldness of speech toward you is great, and great is my glorying in you.

I am filled with comfort; I am exceeding joyful in all our tribulation. For when we came into Macedonia our bodies had no rest, but we were troubled on every side—outside were battles, inside were fears. Nevertheless God, who comforts those who are cast down, comforted us by the arrival of Titus. And not in his coming only, but also through the consolation by which he was comforted by you. He told us about your earnest desire, your mourning, your fervent mind toward me, which caused me to rejoice even more.

For though I saddened you with my letter, I do not repent of it—though I repented of it for a time. For I see that the same letter made you sorry, though it was just for a season. So I rejoice now, not that you were made sorrowful, but that you were sorrowed to the point of repentance. For you were made sorry in a godly manner, such that you might not be damaged by us in anything. For godly sorrow works repentance to salvation, and no regrets, but the sorrow of the world works death. For see how your earnestness resulted in a godly sorrow in you, what diligence it brought about in you——yes, what a desire to clear yourselves, what indignation, what fear, what vehement yearning, what zeal, what punishment! In all things ye have approved yourselves to be clear in this matter.

Therefore, though I wrote to you, I did not do it for the sake of the one who had done the wrong, nor for sake of the one who suffered the wrong, but that our care for you in the sight of God might become evident to you. And therefore we were comforted. In addition to that comfort, we rejoiced greatly at the joy of Titus in that his spirit was refreshed by all of you. For in my boasting of you to him, I was not put to shame. Just as we spoke the truth to you, so also in our boasting about you to Titus was true as well. And his affection for you is great, in that he remembers your obedience, how you received him with fear and trembling. My joy is that I have complete confidence in you in everything.[151]

Though I speak with the tongues of men and of angels, if I do not have love, I am just a clanging gong, or a noisy cymbal. And though I have the gift of prophecy, and understand all mysteries, and have all knowledge; and though I have all faith, such that I could remove mountains, but have not love, I am nothing. And though I give all my goods to feed the poor, and though I give up my body to be burned, and have not love, it profits me nothing. Love is longsuffering, and is kind; love does not envy; love does not promote itself, and is not puffed up. Love does not act rudely, and does not insist on its own way, is not easily provoked, and is not resentful. Love does not rejoice in iniquity, but rejoices rather in the truth. Love bears all things, believes all things, hopes all things, and endures all things. Love never fails——where there are prophecies, they shall fail. Where there are tongues, they shall cease. Where there is knowledge, it shall vanish away. For we know in part, and we prophesy in part. But when that which is perfect has arrived, then that which is partial shall be done away with. When I was a child, I spoke like a child, I understood as a child, I thought as a child does. But when I became a man, I put away such childish things. For now we see in a dim mirror, but then face to face. Now I know partially, but then I shall know even as I am known. And now these three abide——faith, hope, and love, but the greatest of them is love.[152]

So pursue love, and desire the more spiritual gifts, but especially that you might prophesy. For he who speaks in an unknown tongue does not speak to men, but rather to God. For no man understands him because he speaks mysteries in the Spirit. But the one who prophesies speaks to men for their edification, exhortation, and comfort. He who speaks in an unknown tongue edifies himself, while the one who prophesies edifies the church.

A WORD ABOUT
TONGUES

I wish that you all spoke in tongues, but more that you prophesied. For the one who prophesies is greater than the one who speaks in tongues——unless there is an interpretation and the church is edified. Now, brothers, if I come to you speaking with tongues, what profit is that, unless I speak to you by revelation, or with a word of knowledge, or by prophesy, or by doctrine?

Even lifeless instruments, like a pipe or a harp, unless there is a distinction in their sounds, how shall anyone know what is played? And if the trumpet gives an uncertain sound, who will get ready for the battle? So you likewise, unless you speak intelligible words with the tongue, how will anyone know what is said? You will be speaking into the air. There are, as it happens, many kinds of languages in the world, and none without meaning. But if I do not know the meaning of the language, I will be to the one who speaks a barbarian, and he that speaks shall be a barbarian to me.

So then, since you are eager for spiritual gifts, strive to excel in the edification of the church. Let the one who speaks in an unknown tongue pray that he may interpret. For if I pray in an unknown tongue, my spirit prays, but my understanding is fruitless. What then? I will pray with my spirit, and I will pray with my mind also. I will sing with the spirit, and I will sing with the mind also. Otherwise when you bless with the spirit, how shall he who stands in the place of the uninitiated say *amen* at your thanksgiving, since he does not understand what you are saying? For you can give thanks well enough, but the other man is not edified.

I thank my God that I speak in tongues more than all of you. But in the church I would rather speak five words with understanding, that by my speaking I might instruct others also, than to speak ten thousand words in an unknown tongue. Brothers, do not be children in understanding——certainly you should be children when it comes to malice, but in understanding you should be men. In the law it is written, "With men of strange tongues and alien speech I will speak to this people, and yet for all that will they not hear me, says the Lord." Therefore tongues are for a sign, not to those who believe, but rather for those who do not believe. Prophecy, on the other hand, does not serve the unbeliever, but rather those who believe. So therefore if the whole church comes together in one place, and everyone speaks with tongues, and someone comes in as untaught or as an unbeliever, will he not say that you are out of your minds? But if all are prophesying, and an unbeliever or an untaught person comes in, he will be convinced by all. He will be judged by all. The secrets of his heart will be made manifest, and so falling on his face he will worship God, and will testify that God is truly among you.

How is it then, brothers? When you come together, each one of you has a psalm, or a doctrine, or a tongue, or a revelation, or an interpretation. Let everything be done for edification. If any man speak in an unknown tongue, let it be two men, or three at the most, and that in order. Make sure someone interprets. If no interpreter is available, let him keep silence in the church, keeping his tongue between himself and God. Let the prophets speak, two or at the most three, and let the others preside in judgment. If a revelation comes to one who is seated, let the first one give way. For you all may prophesy, one at a time, in order that all might learn, and all might be comforted. For the spirits of the prophets are subject to the prophets. God is not the author of confusion, but of peace, as in all churches of the saints.[153]

GOOD ORDER

Let your women keep silence in the churches——it is not permitted for them to speak. Rather, they are commanded to be in subjection, as the law says. And if they want to learn something, then let them ask their husbands at home. For it is a shame for women to speak in the church. *What?* Did the Word of God originate with you? Or did it come only to you? If any man considers himself a prophet, or a spiritual man, let him acknowledge that the things that I write to you here are the commandments of the Lord. But if any man be ignorant, let him stay that way. Therefore, brothers, earnestly desire that you might prophesy, and do not forbid speaking in tongues. Let everything be done decently and in order.[154]

Let love be without hypocrisy. Abhor that which is evil; cling to what is good. Be kindly affectionate toward one another in brotherly love, in honor giving preference to one another. Do not be sluggish in zeal, be fervent in spirit, serving the Lord. Rejoice in hope, be patient in tribulation, continue constantly in prayer, distribute to the needs of the saints, be given to hospitality. Bless those who persecute you——bless and do not curse. Rejoice with those who rejoice, and weep with those who weep. Be of the same mind toward one another. Do not be haughty, but stoop to men in a humble condition. Do not be wise in your own conceits. Pay back no man evil for evil. Deal honestly in the sight of all men. If it is possible, as far as it concerns you, live in peace with all men.

Dearly beloved, do not take vengeance for yourself, but rather leave room for wrath. For it is written, "Vengeance is mine; I will repay, says the Lord." Therefore if your enemy is hungry, feed him. If he is thirsty, give him a drink. For in doing this you will heap coals of fire on his head. Do not be overcome by evil, but overcome evil with good.[155]

Be imitators of God, as dear children, and walk in love, as Christ also loved us, and gave Himself for us as an offering, and as a sacrifice to God for a sweet smelling aroma. But fornication and every form of uncleanness and covetousness——do not even let it be named among you, as is befitting for saints. Neither should there be filthiness, or foolish chatter, or coarse jokes, which are inappropriate, but rather let there be thanksgiving. For this you know—— no whoremonger, no unclean person, no covetous man, who is an idolater, has any inheritance in the kingdom of Christ and of God. Let no man deceive you with vain words——because of such things the wrath of God is coming upon the children of disobedience. Therefore do not be partakers with them. For you were one time darkness, but now you are light in the Lord——so walk as children of light. For the fruit of the Spirit is found in all goodness and righteousness and truth, and proves what is acceptable to the Lord.

And have no fellowship with the unfruitful works of darkness, but rather reproach them. For it is a shame even to speak of those things which are secretly done by them. But all things that are reproached are revealed by the light, for whatever reveals things is light. Therefore he says, "Awake you sleeper, arise from the dead, and Christ shall give you light." See then that you walk carefully, not like fools, but as wise men, redeeming the time, because the days are evil. Therefore do not be unwise, but understanding what the will of the Lord is.

And do not get drunk with wine, which is dissipation, but rather be filled by the Spirit. Do this speaking to yourselves in psalms, hymns and spiritual songs, singing and making melody in your heart to the Lord, giving thanks always for all things to our God and Father in the name of our Lord Jesus Christ, submitting to one another in the fear of God.[156]

Brothers, if a man is overtaken in a fault, you who are spiritual restore that man in a spirit of gentleness, considering yourself, in case you are tempted also. Bear one another's burdens, and so fulfill the law of Christ. For if a man thinks himself to be something when he is nothing, he deceives himself. Let every man test his own work, and then his basis for joy will be in his own work, and not in the work of another. For every man shall bear his own burden.

Let the one who is taught in the word share all good things with the one who teaches. Do not be deceived—God is not mocked. For whatever a man sows, that is what he will reap. For he who sows to his flesh shall from the flesh reap corruption, but he who sows to the Spirit shall from the Spirit reap everlasting life. And do not let us grow weary in well doing, for in due season we shall come to the harvest, if we do not falter. As we have opportunity, therefore, let us do good to all men, especially for those who are in the household of faith.[157]

Flee youthful lusts, and pursue righteousness, faith, love, and peace, together with those who call on the Lord from a pure heart. But foolish and ignorant questions avoid, knowing that they just perpetuate strife. And the servant of the Lord must not strive; but rather be gentle to all men, able to teach, and patient, in gentleness instructing those who oppose him, if by any chance God might give them repentance to the point where they acknowledge the truth——that they might escape from the snare of the devil, where they are held captive by his will.[158]

Now know this also. In the last days perilous times shall come. For men will be lovers of themselves, covetous, boasters, proud, blasphemers, disobedient to parents, ungrateful, unholy, without natural affection, treacherous, slanderers, without self-control, fierce, despisers of those who are good, traitors, reckless, insolently conceited, lovers of pleasure more than lovers of God. Having a form of godliness, they deny the actual power of it——from this kind of man turn away. For this is the sort that creeps into houses, and entraps silly women laden down with sins, and led astray by various lusts, always learning and never coming to a knowledge of the truth. Now as Jannes and Jambres opposed Moses, so also these men resist the truth. They are men of corrupt mind, and rejected concerning the faith. But they will make it no further——for their folly will be manifest before all men, as happened with Jannes and Jambres.[159]

AUTHORITY AND
SUBMISSION

Let every person be subject to the higher authorities. For there is no authority except from God;
the authorities that exist have been ordained by
God. Whoever therefore resists that authority resists the ap-
pointment of God, and those who resist it will receive condemnation. For rulers are not a terror to good behavior, but
rather to bad. Would you be unafraid of the one in authority? Then do what is good, and you will have his approval.
For he is the servant of God for your good. But if you do
what is evil, be afraid, because he does not bear the sword
in vain. For he is the servant of God, an avenger to execute
wrath upon the evildoer. This is why you must be subject,
not only to avoid wrath, but also for conscience' sake. For
this reason you pay taxes as well——for the authorities are
God's servants, attending constantly to this very thing.[160]

I urge you therefore, first of all, to make supplications, prayers, intercessions, and giving of thanks, for all
men——for kings, and for any who are in authority, so that
we might lead a quiet and peaceable life in all godliness
and honesty. For this is good and acceptable in the sight
of God our Savior, who desires all men to be saved and to
come to the knowledge of the truth. For there is one God,
and one mediator between God and man, the man Christ

Jesus, who gave Himself as a ransom for all, as a testimony at the right time.[161]

Remind the people to be subject to principalities and powers, to obey the magistrate, to be ready for every good work. They should not speak evil of any man, and not be brawlers, but rather gentle, showing all meekness to all men. For we ourselves used to be foolish, disobedient, deceived, serving various lusts and pleasures, living in malice and envy, hateful, and hating one another.[162]

Children, obey your parents in the Lord. This is the right thing. Honor your father and mother   the first commandment with a promise——so that it might go well with you, and that you might live long on the earth.

And you fathers, do not provoke your children to anger, but instead bring them up in the nurture and admonition of the Lord.

Slaves, be obedient to those who are your masters according to the flesh. Do it with fear and trembling, with singleness of heart, as rendered to Christ——not with eye service, as though working to please men, but rather as slaves of Christ, doing the will of God from the heart, offering your service with good will, as to the Lord, and not to men. Know this——whatever good thing any man does, he will receive back in kind from the Lord, whether he is a slave or a free man. And, you masters, do the same things for your slaves, without threats, knowing that you have a master also, who is in heaven, and with Him there is no respect of persons.[163]

Let as many slaves who are under the yoke reckon their own masters as worthy of all honor, so that the name of God and His doctrine will not be blasphemed. And those who have believing masters should not despise them——because they are brothers they should offer good service, because they are faithful and beloved, partakers of the benefit. Teach these things, and exhort in terms of it. If a man teaches otherwise, and disagrees with these wholesome words——even the words of our Lord Jesus Christ——and differs with the teaching in accord with godliness, then that man is a conceited ignoramus, and he dotes on controversy and wrangling with words, out of which arise envy, strife, slander, evil suspicion, and constant quarreling among men who are corrupt in mind, and bereft of the truth, supposing that profit is piety. From such men turn away.[164]

Let every man remain in the same calling in which he was called. Were you called when a slave? Do not mind it . . . but if you have an opportunity for freedom, be sure to take it. For a man called in the Lord as a slave is the Lord's freed man, just as the man called as a freed man is Christ's slave. You were bought with a price, so do not become slaves of men. Brothers, let every man abide with God, whatever his calling.[165]

Render to everyone what is due. Pay tribute to whom tribute is due; custom to whom custom; fear to whom fear; honor to whom honor. Do not owe any man anything, except for the obligation to love one another. For he who loves another has fulfilled the law. For these command-ments, "You shall not commit adultery," "You shall not murder," "You shall not steal," "You shall not bear false witness," "You shall not covet,"——and if there are any other commandments——are all summed in this saying, namely, "You shall love your neighbor as yourself." Love works no harm for his neighbor, which means that love is the fulfilling of the law.[166]

Therefore, though I could be quite bold in Christ to command you in what is required, yet for the sake of love I would rather plead with you——I, Paul, an old man as well as a prisoner for the sake of Jesus Christ. I plead with you for the sake of my child Onesimus, whose father I be-came in my imprisonment. He used to be useless to you, but now is useful both to you and to me. I am sending him back to you, so please receive him as my very heart. I would have rejoiced to keep him here with me so that in *your* place he might have ministered to me in the time of my imprisonment for the gospel. But apart from your consent, I would do nothing so that your gift should not be coerced, but offered willingly. So perhaps this is why he was parted from you for a time, that you might receive him back forever——no longer as a slave, but more than a slave, as a beloved brother, to me especially, but how much more to you, both in the flesh and in the Lord?

So if you count me as a partner, receive him as you would receive me. If he has wronged you, or owes you anything, put that down to my account. I, Paul, am writing this with my own hand——I will pay it back my-self. I do not mention how you owe your very life to me. Truly, brother, let me have some blessing from you in the Lord. Refresh my heart in the Lord.[167]

FREEDOM FROM LUST

And so now, knowing the time, it is high time to wake up from sleep——for our salvation is now nearer than when we first believed. The night is far spent, the day is at hand. Let us therefore throw off the works of darkness, and let us put on the armor of light. Let us walk honestly as in the daytime, not in raves or drunkenness, not in promiscuity or wantonness, not in quarrels or jealousies. But rather put on the Lord Jesus Christ, and make no provision for the flesh, to gratify its lusts.[168]

So it is commonly reported that there is fornication among you, and the kind of fornication that is not even named among the Gentiles——when a man has his father's wife. And you are puffed up about it! Why have you not rather mourned over it, that the one who has done this thing might be removed from among you. For though absent in the body but present in spirit, as if present I have truly already judged the one who has done this. When you are gathered together in the name of our Lord Jesus Christ, and my spirit is present, in the power of our Lord Jesus Christ, you must deliver such a man to Satan for the destruction of the flesh, so that his spirit might be saved in the day of the Lord Jesus. Your boasts are not good. Do you not know that a little leaven leavens the entire lump? Therefore purge the old leaven out, so that you may be a new lump, as you genuinely are unleavened. For Christ, our Passover lamb, has been sacrificed for us. Let us therefore celebrate the feast, not with the old leaven, the leaven of malice and wickedness, but with the unleavened bread of sincerity and truth.

I wrote to you in my epistle not to keep company with fornicators. But I did not mean the fornicators of this world, or with the greedy or fraudulent, or with idolaters, for that would mean you would have to go out of the world. But now I have written to you not to keep company with any man called a brother, if he is a fornicator, or greedy, or an idolater, reviler, drunkard, or a swindler. With someone like that you should not even eat. For what do I have to do in judging outsiders? Do you not judge those who are inside the church? God is the one who judges those outside. So put away the wicked person from among yourselves.[169]

Now concerning virgins I have no command from the Lord, but I give my judgment as one who by the Lord's mercy is faithful. In view of the present distress, I think it is good for a man to remain as he is. Are you bound to a wife? Do not seek to get free. Are you free from a wife? Do not seek a wife. But if you do marry, you have not sinned. And if a virgin marries, she has not sinned. But those who marry will have trouble in the flesh, and I would spare you that.

This is what I mean, brothers. The time is short. From this point on, those who have wives should live as though they did not. And those who weep as though they did not weep. And those who rejoice as though they did not rejoice, and those who buy as though they owned nothing. And those who deal in this world as though they did not deal in it. For the form of this present work is passing away.

I want you free from care. An unmarried man care for the things belonging to the Lord, how he may please the Lord. But the married man cares for the things that are of the world, how he may please his wife. There is also another difference between a wife and a virgin. The unmarried woman cares for the things of the Lord, that she may be holy both in body and in spirit. But the married woman cares for the things of the world, how she may please her husband. Now I say this for your own benefit, and not to constrain you, but only to encourage good order, so that you might attend to the Lord without distraction.

Now if any man believes he is behaving poorly toward his virgin, if she is passing the flower of her age, and it seems necessary, let him do as he wills. He is not sinning; let them marry. At the same time, if he is standing steadfast in his heart, and is under no necessity, having power over his own will, and has settled in his heart that he will keep her as his virgin, he does well also. So then he that marries his virgin does well, and he who refrains from marrying his virgin does even better.

A wife is bound by the law as long as her husband is alive. But if her husband is dead, she is at liberty to marry whom she will——only in the Lord. But she is happier if she remains as she is, at least by my judgment——and in this I believe I have the Spirit of God.[170]

Now further, we plead with you, brothers, and exhort you by the Lord Jesus, that just as you received from us how you ought to walk and to please God, so also you would abound in such things more and more. For you know what commandments we gave you in the Lord Jesus. For this is the will of God, your sanctification, that you should refrain from fornication. Every one of you needs to know how to possess his vessel in sanctification and honor, not in the lust of passionate desire, like the Gentiles do, those who do not know God. No man should go beyond bounds, defrauding his brother in any such matter——because the Lord takes vengeance on all such, as we also have forewarned you and testified. For God has not called us to uncleanness, but to holiness. Therefore he who despises this word does not despise man, but rather God——who has given to us His Holy Spirit.[171]

Therefore I say to the unmarried and widows, it is good for them if they remain the same way I am. But if they cannot contain themselves, then let them marry——it is better to marry than to burn with passion. And to the married my command——and this is not really mine, but the Lord's teaching——let the wife not depart from her husband. But if she departs, let her remain unmarried, or else be reconciled to her husband. And a husband should not put away his wife.

Concerning the others——and this is not the Lord's doctrine, but mine——if any brother has a wife who is not a believer, and she is pleased to live with him, then he should not put her away. And if a woman has a husband who does not believe, and if he is pleased to live with her, then she should not leave him. For the unbelieving husband is sanctified by his wife, and the unbelieving wife is sanctified by her husband——otherwise the children would be unclean, but as it is, they are holy.

But if the unbeliever departs, then let him depart. A brother or a sister is not bound in such cases, for God has called us to peace. For how do you know, O wife, whether you will save your husband? Or how do you know, O man, whether you will save your wife?[172]

AVOIDING WRANGLES

Receive the one who is weak in faith, but not for the sake of dubious disputes. For one man believes that he may eat anything, while another, who is weak in his faith, eats only vegetables. Let not the man who eats despise the one who will not eat, and let not the man who refuses to eat judge the one who does eat——*God* has received him. Who are you to judge another man's servant? To his own master he stands or falls. Yes——he shall be held up, for God is able to make him stand.

One man esteems one day above another; another esteems every day alike. Let every man be fully persuaded in his own mind. He who regards the day regards it before the Lord, and he who does not regard the day, to the Lord he does not regard it. He who eats does so to the Lord, for he gives God thanks, and he who does not eat, to the Lord he refrains from eating, and also gives God thanks.[173]

Therefore, my beloved, as you have always obeyed, not only in my presence, but now much more in my absence, work out your own salvation with fear and trembling——for it is God who works in you both to will and to do His good pleasure. Do everything without grumbling or quarreling, so that you may be blameless and harmless, the sons of God, without fault, in the midst of a crooked and perverse nation, among whom you shine as lights in the world. Do this holding forth the word of life so that I might rejoice in the day of Christ that I have not run in vain, nor labored in vain. Yes, and if I am poured out upon the sacrificial offering of your faith, I am glad in it, and rejoice with you all. For the same reason you are glad also, and rejoice with me.[174]

How do you dare——having an issue with another—— to go to law before the unrighteous instead of before the saints? Do you not know that the saints shall judge the world? And if the *world* will be judged by you, how are you unable to judge these little cases? Do you not know that we are to judge angels? How much more, then, issues that pertain to this life! So then if you have cases pertaining to this life, why not set them before those who are the least in the church? I say this to your shame. Is it really true that there is no wise man among you? No one able to judge between brothers?

But brother goes to court against brother, and all in front of unbelievers. You are already completely at fault just because there are lawsuits in your midst. Why not rather accept the wrong? Why not allow yourselves to be defrauded? But you yourselves do what is wrong, and defraud even your own brothers.

Do you not know that the unrighteous will not inherit the kingdom of God? Do not be deceived. Neither fornicators, nor idolaters, nor adulterers, nor effeminate, nor sodomites, nor thieves, nor the covetous, nor drunkards, nor revilers, nor swindlers, will inherit the kingdom of God. And such were some of you——but you are washed, but you are sanctified, but you are justified in the name of the Lord Jesus, and by the Spirit of our God.[175]

There are many who are rebellious, vain talkers and deceivers, particularly those of the circumcision party. Their mouths need to be stopped because they are subverting entire households——teaching things they should not, and that for the sake of filthy gain.

One of them, a prophet of their own nation, said, "Cretans are always liars, evil beasts, and slow bellies." This testimony is true. Therefore rebuke them sharply so that they might be sound in the faith, not given over to Jewish fables and commandments of men who turn away from the truth. For the pure, all things are pure, but to the defiled and unbelieving, nothing is pure——both mind and conscience are defiled. They profess to know God, but by their works they deny Him. They are deplorable, disobedient, and rejected for any good work.[176]

For no man among us lives to himself, and no man dies to himself. For if we live, we live before the Lord; and if we die, we die before the Lord. So whether we live or die, we are the Lord's. For this purpose Christ both died and rose——He came back to life in order to be the Lord of both the dead and living.[177]

Therefore stand fast in the liberty in which Christ has made us free, and do not be tangled up again with the yoke of bondage. Behold, I Paul say this to you, that if you get circumcised, then Christ profits you nothing. For I testify again that every man who is circumcised becomes a debtor obligated to fulfill the entire law. Christ has become of no effect for you, whichever of you seeks to be justified by the law——you are fallen from grace. For it is through the Spirit that we wait for the hope of righteousness by faith. For in Jesus Christ neither circumcision nor lack of circumcision avails anything, but only faith which works by love.

You were running well. Who came in to hinder you so that you should not obey the truth? This persuasion does not come from the One who called you. Just a little leaven leavens the whole lump. In the Lord, I have confidence in you that you will not be otherwise minded . . . but the one who troubles you will bear his judgment, whoever he might be. Brothers, if I am still preaching circumcision, why am I still suffering persecution? That would remove all the offense of the cross. I wish those who trouble you would cut everything off.

For, brothers, you have been called into liberty. But do not use that liberty as an opportunity for the flesh, but in love serve one another. For the entire law is fulfilled in this one word, "You shall love your neighbor as yourself." But if you bite and devour one another, take care that you not be consumed by one another.[178]

So why do you judge your brother? Or why do you treat your brother with contempt? For we will all stand before the judgment seat of Christ. For it is written, "As I live, says the Lord, every knee shall bow before me, and every tongue shall confess to God." So then each one of us shall give an account of himself to God.

Therefore let us not pass judgment on one another any further, but rather decide to not place a stumbling block or any obstacle in his brother's way. I know and am persuaded in the Lord Jesus that nothing unclean in itself——but it is unclean to anyone who considers it to be unclean. For if your brother is grieved by your food, you are not walking in love. Do not destroy, by means of your food, someone for whom Christ died. Do not let what you consider to be good to be spoken of as evil.[179]

Now I say this——that an heir, as long as he is a child, differs in no way from a slave, even though he owns everything. He is under tutors and guardians until the time appointed by his father. In the same way, we, when we were children, were enslaved by the elemental principles of the world. But when the fullness of time had arrived, God sent forth His Son, born of a woman, and born under the law, in order to redeem those who were under the law, so that we might receive the adoption of sons. And because you are sons, God has sent forth the Spirit of His Son into your hearts, crying, "Abba, Father!" Therefore you are no longer a slave, but a son. And if you are a son, then you are an heir of God through Christ.

When you previously did not know God, you were enslaved by those that were not gods by nature. But now that you have come to know God, or better, are known by God, how is it that you turn back again to the weak and bankrupt elementals, to which you desire again to be in bondage? You observe days, and months, and seasons, and years. I am fearful for you, in that I may have bestowed my labor upon you in vain.[180]

For the kingdom of God is not food and drink, but rather righteousness, peace, and joy in the Holy Spirit. For he who serves Christ in these things is acceptable to God, and is also approved of men. So then let us therefore pursue those things that make for peace and mutual edification. Do not destroy the work of God for the sake of food. All things indeed are pure, but it is sinful for a man who eats and by that gives offense. It is good not to eat meat, or to drink wine, or to do anything that stumbles your brother, or offends him, or weakens him. You have faith? Keep it between yourself and God. Blessed is the man who does not condemn himself through things he approves. Whoever doubts is condemned if eats, because the eating does not come from faith. And whatever does not come from faith is sin.[181]

Therefore let no man judge you in food or in drink, or with regard to a holy day, or because of the new moon, or because of sabbath days. These things are all a shadow of the things to come, the substance of which is Christ. Let no man trick you out of your reward through asceticism and worship of angels, prying into things he has not seen, puffed up for no reason by his carnal mind——not holding to the Head, from whom the entire body, nourished and knit together by ligaments and joints, grows with the increase that God provides.

So if you are dead with Christ to the elemental principles of the world, why, as though still alive to the world, do you submit to its regulations? I mean things like "Do not touch. Do not taste. Do not handle." These things all perish in the using, and are according to the precepts and doctrines of men. These things certainly have a display of wisdom in exalted self-made religion, asceticism, and harshness to the body——but they are no good in checking the flesh.[182]

A RIGHT USE OF LAW

When I left for Macedonia, I urged you to remain in Ephesus, in order that you might charge certain individuals not to teach any other doctrine, nor to pay attention to myths and endless genealogies, which just generate questions, rather than wise edification from God by faith. Now the purpose of this requirement is love from a pure heart, a good conscience, and a genuine faith. Certain individuals, by swerving from this, have wandered off into a vain jangling. They desire to be teachers of the law, not understanding what they are saying, or what they are trying to affirm.

Now we know that the law is good, if a man uses it lawfully. But he must understand this——the law is not intended for a righteous man, but rather for the lawless and disobedient, for the ungodly and for sinners, for the unholy and profane, for murderers of fathers and murderers of mothers, for whoremongers, for sodomites, for slave traders, for liars, for perjurers, not to mention anything else that is contrary to sound doctrine——and all in accordance with the glorious gospel of the blessed God, with which I was entrusted.[183]

Now the Spirit speaks expressly that in the later times some will depart from the faith, giving an ear to lying spirits, and doctrines of demons, speaking hypocritical lies, and with consciences that have been cauterized. They forbid marriage, and command abstinence from food that God created to be received with thanksgiving by any who believe and know the truth. For everything created by God is good, and nothing is to be rejected, provided it is received with thanksgiving. Anything like that is sanctified by the word of God and prayer.

If you remind the brothers of these things, you will be a good servant of Jesus Christ, being trained in the words of faith, and by the good doctrine you have practiced. But reject profane old wives' tales, and instead train yourself for godliness. While bodily exercise has some value, godliness is valuable in every way, as having promise for the present life, not to mention the life to come. This is a faithful saying and worthy of full acceptance. For toward this goal we both labor and suffer reproach, because we trust in the living God, who is the Savior of all men, and especially those who believe. Command and teach these things.[184]

All things are lawful for me, but not everything is helpful. All things are lawful for me, but I will not be enslaved by anything. Food is for stomach, and the stomach is for food, but God will destroy both of them. Now the body is not intended for fornication, but for the Lord——and the Lord for the body. And God has raised up the Lord, and will also raise us up by His own power. Do you not know that your bodies are the members of Christ? Shall I then take the members of Christ, and make them the members of a prostitute? God forbid it. What? Do you not know that the man who is joined to a prostitute is one body with her? For the two, he says, "shall be one flesh." But the man who is joined to the Lord is one spirit with Him. Flee from fornication. Every other sin that a man commits is apart from the body, but the man who commits fornication sins against his own body. What? Do you not know that your body is the temple of the Holy Spirit who is in you, and which you have from God? So you are not your own. For you were bought with a price——therefore glorify God in your body, and in your spirit, which both belong to God.[185]

Therefore having these promises, dearly beloved, let us cleanse ourselves from all filthiness of flesh and spirit, perfecting holiness in the fear of God.[186]

Now as concerning things offered up to idols——we know that we all have knowledge. Knowledge puffs up, but love builds up. And if any man thinks that he knows something, he knows nothing yet as he ought to know. But any man who loves God, that same man is known by Him.

So therefore as concerning eating what has been offered in sacrifice to idols, we know that an idol is nothing in the world, and that there is no other God but One. For though there be many that are called gods, whether in heaven or in earth——as there are many gods, and many lords——for us there is only one God, the Father. From Him are all things, and we are in Him, and there is one Lord Jesus Christ, by whom are all things, and we also by Him.

But not every man has such knowledge. For some with awareness of the idol down to the present eat it *as* a thing offered to an idol, and their conscience being weak is thereby defiled. But meat does not commend us to God. We are no better off if we eat, and if we refrain from eating, we are none the worse. But take care lest somehow this liberty of yours become a stumbling block to those who are weak. For if any man see you, the knowledgeable one, sitting down to eat mean in an idol's temple, will he not, weak conscience and all, be encouraged to eat meat offered to idols? And thus, through *your* knowledge, the weak brother perishes, for whom Christ died. But when you sin against your brothers and wound their weak consciences, you are sinning against Christ. Therefore, if meat makes my brother stumble, I will eat no flesh while the world stands——lest I make my brother stumble.[187]

All things are lawful for me, but not all things are helpful. All things are lawful for me, but not everything edifies. Let no man seek his own good, but rather the good of his brother. Whatever is sold in the meat market may be eaten, without asking questions for the sake of conscience. "For the earth is the Lord's, and the fulness of it." If any unbelievers invite you to a feast, and you are willing to go, then eat whatever is set before you. You need not ask questions for the sake of conscience. But if any man says to you, "This was offered in sacrifice to idols," then refrain from eating. You do not do this for the sake of the one who pointed it out, but for the sake of conscience. "For the earth is the Lord's, and the fullness of it." Now when I say conscience, I do not mean yours, but rather the other man's. For why would my liberty be judged by another man's conscience?

For if I am a partaker by grace, then why am I denounced for something over which I gave thanks? So then, whatever you eat or drink, or whatever else you do, do everything to the glory of God. Give offense to no man, whether Jews or Gentiles, or to the church of God. Even so, I seek to please everyone in all that I do, not seeking my own advantage, but rather the advantage of many, that they may be saved. Be imitators of me, just as I also imitate Christ.[188]

This is how men should think of us, as servants of Christ, and as stewards of the mysteries of God. In addition, it is required of stewards that they be found faithful. But with me it is a trivial thing that I should be judged by you, or in any human tribunal. In fact, I will not even judge myself. I am not aware of any fault in myself, but I am not therefore cleared. The Lord is the One who judges me. Therefore do not declare judgments before the time, prior to the Lord's coming. When He comes, He will bring to light what is now hidden in darkness, and will reveal the motives of the hearts. That is when each will have His commendation from God.

FOOLS FOR CHRIST

I have applied these things in a figure, brothers, to Apollos and myself, and have done it for your sakes. I have done it so that you might learn from us not to think beyond what is written, so that none of you get puffed up against one another. For who makes you distinct from another? And what do you have that you did not receive? Now if you were given it, why do you glory as though you were not given it? Now you are so full! Now you are rich, without our help you have reigned as kings! I wish to God you did reign, so that we might reign together with you. For I think that God has set out the apostles last of all, as men sentenced to die. We have been made a spectacle before the world, before angels and men.

We are fools for Christ's sake, but you are so wise in Christ. We are weak, but you are strong. You are honorable; we are despised. Down to the present hour we both hunger and thirst. We are naked, we are buffeted, and we are homeless. And we labor, working with our own hands. When reviled, we return a blessing. When persecuted, we suffer through it. When defamed, we entreat. Down to the present, we are made the filth of the world, and are the scrapings from the bottom of everything.

I do not write these things to shame you, but rather to admonish you as my beloved children. For though you have had ten thousand school guides in Christ, yet you have not had many fathers——for in Christ Jesus I have begotten you through the gospel.

Therefore I plead with you, be imitators of me. This is the reason I sent Timothy to you, my beloved and faithful son in the Lord. He will remind you of my ways in Christ, as I teach everywhere in every church.

Now some are insolent, as though I were not coming to you. But I *will* come to you soon, if the Lord wills it, and discover the power of these insolent ones, and not their words. For the kingdom of God is not made up of words but in power. What would you rather? Shall I come to you with a rod, or with love and a spirit of gentleness?[189]

Now concerning brotherly love, you do not need for me to write to you. For you yourselves have been taught by God to love each other. And in fact you do love all the brothers throughout all Macedonia. We plead with you, brothers, to increase in this love more and more. Pursue a quiet life, minding your own business, and work with your own hands, as we required of you. If you do this, you can walk honestly before outsiders, and be able to take care of yourselves.[190]

MEN AND WOMEN

Those of us who are strong ought to bear with the infirmities of the weak, and not to please ourselves. Let every one of us please his neighbor for his good and edification. For even Christ did not please Himself, but, as it is written, "The reproaches of those who reproached you fell on me." For whatever things were written in earlier times were written for our learning, so that through the patience and comfort of the Scriptures we might have hope.[191]

But you should continue in the things which you have learned and have been assured of, knowing from whom you learned them. From childhood you have known the Holy Scriptures, which are able to make you wise to salvation through faith which is in Christ Jesus. All Scripture is given by inspiration of God, and is profitable for teaching, for reproof, for correction, for instruction in righteousness, with the result that the man of God might be complete, thoroughly equipped for all good works.[192]

Now may the God of patience and consolation grant that you will be likeminded toward one another according to Christ Jesus——that you might with one mind and one mouth glorify God, meaning the Father of our Lord Jesus Christ.[193]

Wives, submit to your own husbands, as to the Lord. For the husband is the head of the wife, just as Christ is the head of the church and the savior of the body. Therefore as the church is subject to Christ, so should the wives be to their own husbands in everything. Husbands, love your wives, just as Christ loved the church, and gave Himself for it——so that He might sanctify and cleanse it with the washing of water by the word. He would do this in order that He might present it to Himself as a glorious church, without spot or wrinkle, or any such thing, but that it should be holy and without blemish. So men ought to love their wives as their own bodies. He who loves his wife loves himself. No man ever hated his own flesh, but nourishes and cherishes it, even as the Lord does the church——for we are members of His body, of His flesh, and of His bones. "For this reason a man shall leave his father and mother, and shall be joined unto his wife, and they two shall be one flesh." This is a great mystery, but I am speaking concerning Christ and the church. So then, let every one of you in particular so love his wife as himself, and let the wife see that she honors her husband.[194]

So then, wives, submit yourselves to your own husbands, as is fitting in the Lord. Husbands, love your wives, and do not be harsh with them. Children, obey your parents in everything, for this is well pleasing to the Lord. Fathers, do not provoke your children to anger, lest they become discouraged. Slaves, obey your earthly masters in all things, not as though being watched, as man-pleasers, but rather in sincerity of heart, fearing God. And whatever you do, do it heartily, as before the Lord, and not before men——knowing that it is from the Lord you will receive the reward of your inheritance. You are serving the Lord Christ. But he who does wrong shall be recompensed for that wrong he has done, and there will be no respect of persons.[195]

I therefore wish that men pray everywhere, lifting up holy hands, without anger or disputing. In the same way, that women adorn themselves in respectable dress, with modest demeanor and decorum——and not with braided hair, or gold, or pearls, or costly clothing. Rather I would that they be adorned——as befits women who profess godliness——with good works.

Let a woman learn quietly with a submissive spirit. I do not allow a woman to teach or to wield authority over a man, but rather to remain quiet. For Adam was formed first, and then Eve. And Adam was not the one deceived, but the woman was deceived and became a transgressor. Nevertheless she shall be saved through childbearing, if they continue in faith and love and holiness, with self-control.[196]

Now concerning the things you wrote about. It is good for a man to refrain from sexual relations with a woman. Nevertheless, in order to avoid fornication, each man should have his own wife, and each woman should have her own husband. Let the husband render to his wife what she is due, and the wife should do the same for her husband. The wife does not have authority over her own body, but her husband does. And in the same way, the husband does not have authority over *his* own body, but his wife does. So do not defraud one another, unless by mutual consent for a time, in order to devote yourselves to fasting and prayer. But then come together again, lest Satan tempt you because of your lack of self-control. I say this by way of concession, and not as a commandment. I wish that all men were as I am in this. But each man has his own gift from God——one has this gift, and another has that.[197]

Now I commend you, brothers, for remembering me in everything, and for maintaining the traditions as I delivered them to you. But I desire that you understand that the head of every man is Christ, and the head of the woman is the man, and the head of Christ is God.

Every man who prays or prophesies with his head covered dishonors his head. And every woman who prays or prophesies with her head uncovered dishonors her head——that would be tantamount to her head being shaved. For if the woman is not covered, then let her be shorn. But if it is shameful for a woman to be shorn or shaven, then let her be covered. A man ought not to cover his head, inasmuch as he is the image and glory of God. But the woman is the glory of the man.

For the man is not of the woman, but the woman of the man. Neither was the man created for the woman, but rather the woman for the man. For this reason the woman ought to have authority on her head——because of the angels. At the same time, the man is not apart from the woman, and the woman is not apart from the man in the Lord. For as the woman is of the man, even so is every man from the woman; and all things are from God.

Judge for yourselves. Is it seemly for a woman to pray to God uncovered? Does not nature itself teach you that if a man has long hair, it is a shame to him? And if a woman has long hair, it is a glory for her. For her hair was given to her for a covering. If anyone is disposed to be contentious, we have no such custom, and neither do the churches of God.[198]

But you must teach those things that accord with sound doctrine. Elderly men should be sober, dignified, temperate, sound in faith, in love, and in steadfastness. The elderly women, in the same way, should be reverent in their behavior, not slanderers, not given over to wine, and teachers of good things. That way they may teach the younger women to love their husbands and children, to be sober, discreet, chaste, busy at home, good, obedient to their own husbands, so that the Word of God will not be slandered.

WALKING WORTHY

I n the same way, exhort the young men to be self-con-
trolled. In everything show yourself to be a model of
good works. In your teaching show integrity, dignity,
honesty, and sound speech that cannot be condemned, so
that an adversary might be put to shame, finding nothing
evil to say about you.

Exhort the slaves to be obedient to their own masters, trying to please them in everything, without talking
back. They should not pilfer, but rather show true fidel-
ity, so that they might adorn the doctrine of God our
Savior in everything.[199]

Masters, give to your slaves what is just and equitable,
knowing that you also have a Master in heaven.[200]

Now we command you, brothers, in the name of our
Lord Jesus Christ, that you withdraw yourselves from every brother who walks in a disorderly way, and not according to the tradition you received from us. For you yourselves know how you ought to imitate us, for we did not
behave in an irresponsible way among you. And neither
did we eat any man's bread without payment, but worked
night and day with toil and labor, so that we might not
be burdensome to any of you. It was not because we did
not have the authority, but rather in our behavior to give
you an example to imitate. For even when we were with

you, we commanded you this: if someone is not willing to work, then neither should he eat. For we hear that there are some among you who walk in a disorderly way, not working at all, but are rather busybodies. Now for those who are this way, we command and exhort in our Lord Jesus Christ, that they do their work quietly, and earn their own way. But as for you, brothers, do not grow weary in doing good. If a man does not obey our words in this letter, make a mark of that man, and have no dealings with him, so that he might be ashamed. And yet do not count him as an enemy, but caution him as a brother.[201]

Therefore welcome one another, as Christ welcomed you, to the glory of God. Now I say that Jesus Christ became a minister to the circumcised to demonstrate God's truthfulness, so that He might confirm the promises made to the fathers. And He also did this so that the Gentiles might glorify God for His mercy. As it is written, "For this reason I will praise you among the Gentiles, and sing to Your name." And again He says, "Rejoice, O Gentiles, with His people." And again, "Praise the Lord, all you Gentiles, and let all peoples praise Him." And also Isaiah said, "The root of Jesse will come, and He will arise to rule the Gentiles; in Him the Gentiles will trust."

Now may the God of hope fill you with all joy and peace in believing, so that you might abound in hope, through the power of the Holy Spirit.

I myself am convinced concerning you, my brothers, that you are filled with goodness, filled with all knowledge, and able also to counsel one another. At the same time, brothers, I have written you very boldly as a reminder, because of the grace that was given to me by God. This was so that I should be a minister of Jesus Christ to the Gentiles, in the priestly ministry of the gospel of God, so that the offering up of the Gentiles might be acceptable, being sanctified by the Holy Spirit.[202]

Only let your manner of life be worthy of the gospel of Christ, so that whether I come to see you, or am absent, I might hear of you that you are standing fast in one spirit, with one mind striving shoulder to shoulder for the faith of the gospel. And that I might hear you are frightened in no way by your adversaries. This is a plain token to them of their destruction, but of your salvation, and that from God. For it has been given to you, for the sake of Christ, not only that you believe in Him, but also to suffer for His sake——as you are in the midst of the same conflict you saw in me, and now hear is still with me.[203]

I therefore have reason to glory in my work for God, through Jesus Christ. For I will not undertake to speak of anything apart from what Christ has worked through me, in order to bring the Gentiles to obedience——through word and deed, through the power of signs and wonders, through the power of the Spirit of God. So from Jerusalem, and around to Illyricum, I have fully preached the gospel of Christ. And so I have made it a point to preach the gospel, not where Christ was already named——lest I build on another man's foundation——but as it is written, "Those who were never told of Him will see, and those who have not heard will understand."

For this reason I have been frequently hindered from coming to you. But now, since there is no room for more work in this place, and because I have had a great desire for years to come to you, I hope to visit you on my way to Spain, and to be helped on my journey there, after I have been blessed by your company for a time. But for now, I am going to Jerusalem to bring help to the saints. For Macedonia and Achaia were pleased to make a contribution for the poor among the Jerusalem saints. They were pleased to do it, and moreover, they owe it to them. For if the Gentiles have been enabled to partake of their spiritual things, then they have an obligation to return service in material things. So therefore when I have finished this task, and have delivered this offering, I will come visit you on my way to Spain. And I am sure that when I come to you, I will come in the fullness of the blessing of the gospel of Christ.[204]

Continue faithfully in prayer, and be watchful in it with thanksgiving. As you do, pray also for us, that God might open for us a door for speaking, to declare the mystery of Christ——which is why I am in prison. Pray that I would be clear, as I ought to be. Walk in wisdom concerning outsiders, making the best use of the time. Let your speech be always gracious, seasoned with salt, so that you might know how you ought to answer every man.[205]

Let no man despise your youth, but rather be an example for the believers——in speech, in your way of life, in love, in spirit, in faith, in purity. Until I arrive, give attention to the reading of Scripture, to exhortation, and to teaching. Do not neglect the gift that you have, which was given you by prophecy, when the presbytery laid hands on you. Meditate on these things. Give yourself entirely to them so that everyone can mark your progress. Pay close attention to yourself, and to your teaching. Continue in them, for by doing so you will save both yourself and those who hear you.

Do not rebuke an older man, but exhort him as you would a father——and the younger men as brothers, the older women as mothers, the younger women as sisters with complete purity.

Honor widows who are genuine widows. But if any widow has children or grandchildren, let them learn to show piety at home first, and thus to pay back their parents, which is good and acceptable before God. Now the woman who is a genuine widow, and all alone, trusts in God and continues in supplications and prayers night and day. But if she lives for pleasure, she is dead while still alive.

Command these things so that they may be blameless. But if anyone does not provide for his own, and especially for members of his own household, he has denied the faith and is worse than an unbeliever.

Do not enroll a widow unless she is at least sixty-years-old, having been the wife of one husband, and having reputation for good works——if she has brought up children, if she has shown hospitality, if she has washed the feet of saints, if she has relieved the afflicted, and if she has diligently pursued every good work. But do not enroll the younger widows, for when their sensuality draws them away from Christ, they will want to marry. Thus they are condemned, having left their former faith. On top of everything, they learn idleness, wandering from house to house. And not only are they idle, but also tattlers and busybodies, saying things they should not. I therefore desire the younger widows marry, bear children, manage their homes, and give the adversary no opportunity for slander. For some are already turned aside to follow Satan. So then, if any believing man or woman has kin who are widows, let them provide the relief. Do not let the church be burdened with it, so that the church may provide for those who are genuine widows.[206]

I charge you before God, and before the Lord Jesus Christ, who will judge the living and the dead, and by His appearing and His kingdom——preach the word; be prepared in season and out of season; reprove, rebuke, exhort with thorough patience and teaching. For the time will come when they will not endure sound teaching, but with itching ears they will pile up teachers to cater to their lusts, and they shall turn away from the truth and wander off into fables. But as for you, be vigilant, endure hardship, do the work of an evangelist, and fill out your ministry.

For I am ready to be poured out as a libation, and the time of my departure is at hand. I have fought the good fight, I have finished my race, I have kept the faith. Hereafter a crown of righteousness is laid up for me, which the Lord, the righteous judge, will award me on that day. And not to me only, but also for all those who have loved His appearing.[207]

Now I plead with you, brothers, for the sake of the Lord Jesus Christ, and by the love of the Spirit, that you strive together with me in your prayers to God for me. Pray that I may be delivered from those in Judea who do not believe, and that my service for Jerusalem may be accepted by the saints there, and that by the will of God I may come to you with joy, and may be refreshed in your presence. May the God of peace be with you all. Amen.[208]

Do not drink just water, but use a little wine for the sake of your stomach and your frequent maladies. The sins of some men are flagrant, going before them to judgment, while other men's sins are dragged behind them. In the same way, the good works of some men are obvious beforehand, and even those which are less conspicuous cannot be successfully hidden.[209]

FAREWELLS AND
BENEDICTIONS

I commend Phoebe our sister to you, a servant of the church which is at Cenchrea. Receive her in the Lord, as befits saints, and assist her in whatever help she needs from you. For she has been a great help to many, and to me as well.

Greet Priscilla and Aquila, my helpers in Christ Jesus. They risked their necks for my life——not only do I thank them, but so do all the churches of the Gentiles. In the same way, greet the church that meets in their house.

Greet my well beloved Epaenetus, the first convert to Christ in Achaia. Greet Mary, who spent much labor on us. Greet Andronicus and Junia, my kinsmen, and my fellow prisoners, who are known among the apostles, and who were in Christ before I was. Greet Ampliatus, my beloved in the Lord. Greet Urbanus, our co-laborer in Christ, and also my beloved Stachys. Greet Apelles, a man approved in Christ. Greet those who are from the household of Aristobulus. Greet my kinsman Herodion. Greet those who are from the household of Narcissus, those who are in the Lord. Greet Tryphena and Tryphosa, who labor in the Lord. Greet the beloved Persis, who labored greatly in the Lord. Greet Rufus, chosen in the Lord, and also his mother——a mother to me as well. Greet

Asyncritus, Phlegon, Hermas, Patrobas, Hermes, along with the brothers who are with them. Greet Philologus, and Julia, Nereus, and his sister, and Olympas, and all the saints who are with them. Greet one another with a holy kiss. The churches of Christ greet you.[210]

Tychicus, who is a beloved brother, will explain my situation to you. He is a faithful minister and fellow servant in the Lord, and I sent him to you for the same reason, that he might know how you are doing, and encourage your hearts. I sent him along with Onesimus, a faithful and beloved brother, who is one of you. They will let you know all the things that are happening here. Aristarchus my fellow prisoner greets you, and Marcus, cousin to Barnabas——concerning whom you received instructions, that if he comes to you, *receive* him——and Jesus, who goes by Justus. They are the only ones from the circumcision party who are my fellow workers in the kingdom of God, and have been a comfort to me. Epaphras, who is one of you, a servant of Christ, greets you. He is always laboring fervently for you in his prayers, that you might stand perfect and complete in all the will of God. For I can testify concerning him that he has a great zeal for you, along with those are in Laodicea, and those in Hierapolis.

Luke, the beloved physician, and Demas, greet you. Greet the brothers who are in Laodicea, and Nympha, together with the church which is in her house. And when this letter is read among you, make sure that it is also read in the church of the Laodiceans, and that you also read the letter sent to them. And tell Archippus that he must take heed to the ministry which he has received in the Lord, that he fulfills it.[211]

Now I plead with you, brothers, mark those who cause divisions and offenses contrary to the teaching which you have learned, and avoid them. For they are those who do not serve our Lord Jesus Christ, but rather their own belly, and by good words and fair speeches deceive the hearts of the simple. For your obedience is known to everyone. I rejoice therefore on your behalf——but want you to be wise in what is good, and simple concerning evil.[212]

Finally, my brothers, be strong in the Lord, and in the strength of His might. Put on the complete armor of God, so that you might be able to stand against the wiles of the devil. For we do not wrestle against flesh and blood, but against principalities, against powers, against the rulers of the darkness of this world, against spiritual wickedness in high places. Therefore take up for yourselves the whole armor of God, so that you might be able to withstand in the evil day, and having done all, to *stand*. Stand therefore, having fastened on the belt of truth, and having put on the breastplate of righteousness. Put on, as shoes for your feet, the readiness brought by the gospel of peace. And above all, take up the shield of faith, with which you will be able to quench all the fiery darts of the wicked one. And put on the helmet of salvation, and take up the sword of the Spirit, which is the word of God. And pray always in the Spirit, with all prayers and supplications. With this in mind, keep watch with all perseverance and supplication for all the saints.

And pray for me, that free utterance might be given to me, that I may open my mouth boldly, to make known the mystery of the gospel, for which I am an ambassador in chains, that I might speak boldly, the way I ought to speak.[213]

And the God of peace will soon bruise Satan under your feet. The grace of our Lord Jesus Christ be with you. Amen.[214]

Therefore, my son, you be strong in the grace that is in Christ Jesus. And the things that you have heard from me before many witnesses, the same things entrust to faithful men, who will be able in turn to teach others. So therefore you should endure hardness, like a good soldier of Jesus Christ. No man going to war entangles himself with civilian affairs because he wants to please the one who enlisted him to be a soldier. And an athlete is not crowned unless he strives according to the rules. And hard-working farmers should be the first partakers of the harvest. Consider what I am saying, and the Lord will give you insight into all of it.[215]

So I rejoiced greatly in the Lord that now finally you have renewed your care for me——not that you did not care, but rather that you lacked opportunity. Not that I am speaking from a position of want because I have learned contentment regardless of my condition. I know both how to be abased and how to abound. Everywhere and in all things I have been taught to be full and to be hungry, both to abound and to go without. I can do all things through Christ who strengthens me. At the same time you have done well, sharing with me in my troubles. Now you Philippians know that in the beginning of the gospel, when I departed from Macedonia, no church partook with me in the matter of giving and receiving, but you only. For even when I was in Thessalonica you gave over and again to my needs. I say this, not angling for a gift, but I do desire the fruit that may abound to your account. I have all I need, and more. I am full, having received from Epaphroditus the gifts which were sent from you, a fragrant offering, a sacrifice acceptable and well pleasing to God. But my God shall supply all your needs according to His riches in glory by Christ Jesus. Now to God our Father be glory forever and ever. Amen.[216]

Charge those who are rich in this present world not to be lofty, or to trust in unstable riches, but rather in the living God, who richly gives all things to enjoy. Teach them to do good, to be rich in good deeds, ready to be generous, eager to share——which will lay up treasure for themselves as a good foundation for the time to come, in order that they might take hold of eternal life.[217]

Philemon, make sure to greet Epaphras, my fellow prisoner in Christ Jesus——and Marcus, Aristarchus, Demas, Lucas, my co-workers.[218]

Having confidence in your obedience I wrote to you, knowing that you will do even more than I ask. In addition, please prepare lodging for me, as I trust that through your prayers I will soon be restored to you.[219]

Timothy, my fellow worker, greets you, as do Lucius, Jason, and Sosipater, my kinsmen, salute you.[220]

But I trust the Lord Jesus to send Timothy to you shortly, so that I might be encouraged by news of you. For I have no man as likeminded as he is, who will be sincerely concerned for your welfare. For everyone seeks his own interest, and not those of Jesus Christ. But you know his tested worth, how as a son with his father he has served with me in the gospel. I hope therefore to send him presently, just as soon as I see how it goes with me. And I also trust in the Lord that I also will come to you soon.

I also thought it was necessary to send Epaphroditus to you, my brother and co-laborer and fellow soldier—not to mention your messenger and minister to my needs. I sent him because he was longing for you all, and was distressed because you had heard that he was sick. And indeed he was sick, next to death. But God had mercy on him, and not simply on him, but on me as well, lest I should have sorrow upon sorrow. So I was eager to send him so that you might rejoice upon seeing him again, and that I might be free from anxiety. Receive him therefore in the Lord with joy, and honor men like that, because he came close to dying for the work of Christ, risking his life in order to fill up what was lacking in your service for me.[221]

Now concerning the collection for the saints, just as I instructed the churches of Galatia, you must do the same. On the first day of each week, let each one of you set aside something, as God has prospered him, so that there are no collections when I arrive. And when I come, I will send whoever you commission by letter, in order to send your gift to Jerusalem. And if it seems fitting for me to go also, then they shall be my companions.[222]

Therefore, my brothers, whom I love and yearn for, my joy and crown, stand fast in the Lord, my beloved. I plead with Euodia and I plead with Syntyche to be likeminded in the Lord. And I entreat you also, true companion, to help those women who labored with me in the gospel, together with Clement, and with the rest of my fellow laborers, whose names are in the book of life.[223]

But since we were separated from you for a brief time, brothers, in person not in heart, we sought more eagerly and with great desire to see you face to face. We would have come to you——I, Paul, over and again——but Satan hindered us. For what is our hope or joy or crown of rejoicing in the presence of our Lord Jesus Christ at His coming? Is it not you? For you are our glory and joy.

Therefore when we could take it no longer, we were willing to be left at Athens alone, and we sent Timothy, our brother and co-worker with God, and our fellow laborer in the gospel of Christ, to establish and encourage you in your faith, so that no man should be unsettled by these afflictions. For you yourselves know that we are destined for this kind of thing.[224]

I Tertius, the one who wrote this epistle, greet you in the Lord. My host Gaius, not to mention host of the whole church, greets you. Erastus the city chamberlain greets you, and also Quartus a brother. The grace of our Lord Jesus Christ be with you all. Amen.[225] The grace of our Lord Jesus Christ be with your spirit. Amen.[226]

Now I want you to understand, brothers, that the things which happened to me have actually worked out for the advancement of the gospel. It has become evident throughout the imperial guard and elsewhere that my chains are for the sake of Christ. And many of our brothers in the Lord, made confident by my chains, have been much more bold to declare the word without timidity. Now some indeed preach Christ out of envy and strife, but others from good will. The former preach Christ of striving ambition, not genuinely, hoping to create extra trouble for me in my bonds. The latter do it out of love, knowing that I am appointed for the defense of the gospel. What then? Notwithstanding, either way, whether in pretense or in truth, Christ is still preached—and I rejoice in that, yes, and I will rejoice.

For I know that this will result in my deliverance— through your prayer and the aid of the Spirit of Jesus Christ. This is according to my earnest expectation and hope, that I shall be ashamed in nothing, but that with all boldness, as always, Christ shall be honored in my body, whether in life or by death. For to me to live is Christ and to die is gain. Now if I live in the flesh, this means fruitful work. But what to choose, I do not know. For I am torn between the two, wanting on the one hand to depart and be with Christ, which is far better, or on the other hand to remain in the flesh, which is more helpful for you. And in this confidence, I know that I shall remain with you all, and continue for your progress and joy in faith. This is so you may have good reason for rejoicing in Jesus Christ through me coming to you again.[227]

So that you may know my work, and how I am doing, Tychicus, a beloved brother and faithful minister in the Lord, will bring you abreast in all things. I have sent him to you for this same purpose, that you might know our affairs, and that he might comfort your hearts. So peace to the brothers, and love with faith, from God the Father and the Lord Jesus Christ. Grace be with all those who love our Lord Jesus Christ in sincerity. Amen.[228]

Greet every saint in Christ Jesus. The brothers who are with me greet you. All the saints greet you, particularly those who are of Caesar's household. The grace of our Lord Jesus Christ be with all of you. Amen.[229]

For I really want you to know the great conflict I have for you, and for those in Laodicea, and for all those who have not seen me face-to-face. I want their hearts to be comforted and knit together in love, attaining to all the riches of a full assurance of understanding, to the acknowledgement of the mystery of God, and of the Father, and of Christ. In Him are hidden all the treasures of wisdom and knowledge. And I say this lest any man should deceive you with enticing words. For though I am absent in the body, yet I am with you in the spirit, rejoicing as

I observe your order, and the steadfastness of your faith in Christ. As you have therefore received Christ Jesus as Lord, so walk in Him——rooted and built up in Him, and established in the faith, as you have been taught, abounding in it with thanksgiving.[230]

You can see how large the letters that I have formed for you, written with my own hand.[231] Now as many as walk according to this rule, let peace be upon them, and mercy, and also upon the Israel of God. From this point on let no man trouble me, for I bear in my body the marks of the Lord Jesus. Brothers, the grace of our Lord Jesus Christ be with your spirit. Amen.[232]

Rejoice in the Lord always——and I will say it again, *rejoice.* Let your gentleness be known to all men. The Lord is at hand. Be anxious about nothing, but in everything, by prayer and supplication with thanksgiving, let your requests be made known to God. And the peace of God, which passes all understanding, will guard your hearts and minds through Christ Jesus.

Finally, brothers, whatever things are true, whatever things are honest, whatever things are just, whatever things are pure, whatever things are lovely, whatever things have a good report——if there is any virtue, or any praise, meditate on such things. Those things which you have learned, received, heard, and seen in me, do those things. And the God of peace will be with you.[233]

Now we exhort you, brothers, warn those who are unruly, comfort the discouraged, lift up the weak, be patient toward all men. See that no one renders evil for evil to any man, but always follow what is good, whether among yourselves, or before all men. Rejoice always. Pray without ceasing. In everything give thanks, for this is the will of God in Christ Jesus concerning you. Do not quench the Spirit. Do not despise prophesying. Test everything, and hold fast that which is good. Refrain from every form of evil. And may the God of peace sanctify you entirely, and I pray to God that your whole spirit and soul and body will be preserved blameless until the coming of our Lord Jesus Christ. Faithful is the One who calls you, and He will do it.

Brothers, pray for us. Greet all the brothers with a holy kiss. I charge you by the Lord to read this letter to all the holy brothers. The grace of our Lord Jesus Christ be with you. Amen.[234]

Hold firmly to the pattern of sound words that you heard from me, in the faith and love which are in Christ Jesus. Keep the good deposit which was entrusted to you, by the Holy Spirit who dwells in us. You know that all who were in Asia have turned away from me, including Phygellus and Hermogenes. May the Lord show mercy to the house of Onesiphorus, for he frequently refreshed me and was not ashamed of my chains. When he was in Rome, he searched for me very diligently until he found me. May the Lord grant mercy to him from the Lord in that day. And you know very well how many ways he ministered to us at Ephesus.[235]

Do every effort to come to me soon. For Demas, out of love for this present world, has forsaken me and departed to Thessalonica. Crescens is gone to Galatia, and Titus to Dalmatia. Only Luke is with me. Get Mark and bring him with you, for he is very useful to me in the ministry. I have sent Tychicus to Ephesus. When you come, bring the cloak that I left at Troas with Carpus, along with the books——but especially the parchments.

Alexander the coppersmith did me a lot of harm—— may the Lord pay him out according to his works. You be wary of him also, for he has opposed our teaching very strongly. At my first defense, no one stood with me—— everyone scattered. I pray to God that it not be laid to their charge. Nevertheless the Lord stood with me and strengthened me, so that through me the message might be fully known, and that all the Gentiles might hear it. I was delivered out of the mouth of the lion. And the Lord will deliver me from every evil work, and will preserve me to His heavenly kingdom——to whom be glory for ever and ever. Amen.[236]

O full of all subtlety and all mischief, you child of the devil, you enemy of all righteousness, will you not cease perverting the right ways of the Lord? So now, look, the hand of the Lord is upon you. You will be blind, not see-ing the sun for a time.[237]

Greet Priscilla and Aquila, and the household of Onesiphorus. Erastus remained at Corinth, but I left Trophimus sick at Miletus. Make every effort to come before winter. Eubulus greets you, and Pudens, and Linus, and Claudia, and all the brothers. The Lord Jesus Christ be with your spirit. Grace be with you. Amen.[238]

When I send Artemas to you, or Tychicus, make sure to come to me in Nicopolis——I have decided to winter there. Help Zenas the lawyer and Apollos on their way, making sure they lack nothing. And let our people learn how to give themselves to good works in urgent cases, so that they are not unfruitful. Everyone with me sends greetings to you. Greet those who love us in the faith. Grace be with all of you. Amen.[239]

Now to Him who has the power to establish you according to my gospel, and the preaching of Jesus Christ, according to the revelation of the mystery, which was kept hidden since the world began, but which is now made manifest, and by the Scriptures of the prophets, according to the commandment of the everlasting God, made known to all nations to the obedience of faith, to the only wise God, be glory through Jesus Christ for ever. Amen.[240]

O Timothy, keep the deposit entrusted to you. Avoid profane and vain babblings, and the contradictions of knowledge——so called *knowledge*——which some by professing have wandered off from the faith. Grace be with you. Amen.[241]

Remember Jesus Christ, of the seed of David, was raised from the dead according to my gospel. For this I endure trouble, as an evil doer, even to chains. But the Word of God is not bound. Therefore I endure everything for the sake of the elect, so that they also may obtain the salvation which is in Christ Jesus, with eternal glory. It is a faithful saying: If we have died with Him, we shall also live with Him. If we suffer, we shall also reign with Him. If we deny Him, He will also deny us. If we are faithless, He remains faithful for He cannot deny Himself.[242]

Now I am passing through Macedonia, and I will visit you when I do. And it may be that I will stay with you, and perhaps winter with you, so that you might help me on my journey wherever I go. For I do not want to see you just in passing now, but rather to remain with you a while, if the Lord permits. But I will remain here at Ephesus until Pentecost——for a wide open door for effectual ministry has opened up for me, and there are many adversaries.

Now if Timothy comes, make him feel at home, for he is doing the Lord's work, just as I am. Let no one despise him, but help him come to me in peace when he comes with the brothers. Concerning our brother Apollos, I greatly desired that he come to you with the brothers, but he did not want to come at this time. But he will come when the time is convenient for him. Keep watch, stand fast in the faith, acquit yourselves like men, be strong. Let everything be done in love.

Now I plead with you, brothers——you know the household of Stephanas, the first fruits of Achaia, and how they have given themselves to the ministry of the saints——to submit to people like this, and to all who help us, laboring with us. I rejoiced at the coming of Stephanas and Fortunatus and Achaicus. All that was lacking on your end they have supplied, for they refreshed both my spirit and yours. Recognize people who are like this.

The churches of Asia greet you. Aquila and Priscilla greet you warmly in the Lord, along with the church that meets in their house. All the brothers greet you. Greet one another with a holy kiss.

I, Paul, write this greeting in my own hand. If anyone does not love the Lord Jesus Christ, then let him be cursed. Lord Jesus, come. The grace of our Lord Jesus Christ be with you. My love to all of you in Christ Jesus. Amen.[243]

So therefore we always pray for you, that our God would consider you worthy of this calling, and fulfill all the good pleasure of His goodness, and the work of faith with power, that the name of our Lord Jesus Christ may be glorified in you, and you in Him, according to the grace of our God and the Lord Jesus Christ.[244]

Now may the Lord of peace Himself give you peace in every way and at all times. The Lord be with you all. I, Paul, write this with my own hand—the marker of all my letters. This is how I write. The grace of our Lord Jesus Christ be with you all. Amen.[245]

Do you not know that all the runners compete in the race, but only one receives the prize? So run, that you may obtain the prize. And every athlete who strives for the mastery is disciplined in all things. Now they do it to obtain a perishable wreath, but we do it for an imperishable one. So this is how I run, not uncertainly. This is how I fight, not as one shadow boxing. But I keep my body under, bringing it into subjection, lest that by any means, after having preached to others, I myself might be disqualified.[246]

Fight the good fight of faith. Lay hold on eternal life, which you were called to, and concerning which you have made a good confession before many witnesses. I give you this charge in the sight of God, who gives life to all things, and before Christ Jesus, who before Pontius Pilate made a good confession——keep this commandment unblemished and without reproach until the appearing of our Lord Jesus Christ. He will be made manifest at the right time, He who is the blessed and only Ruler, the King of kings, and Lord of lords, who alone has immortality, and who dwells in un-approachable light, whom no man has seen, nor can see, to whom be honor and power everlasting. Amen.[247]

Now to the King eternal, immortal, invisible, the only wise God, be honor and glory forever and ever. Amen. This charge I commit to you, my son Timothy, according to the prophecies which were made about you earlier, that in accordance with them you might wage a good warfare. I charge that you do this, holding the faith and a good conscience. By not doing this some have made a ship-wreck concerning the faith, including Hymenaeus and Alexander, whom I have delivered over to Satan so that they might learn not to blaspheme.[248]

I write all these things hoping to come to you shortly. But if I am delayed, you will still know how you ought to conduct yourself in the house of God, which is the church of the living God, the pillar and ground of the truth. And without dispute, the mystery of godliness is great——God was made manifest in the flesh, justified in the Spirit, seen by angels, preached to the Gentiles, believed on in the world, and received up into glory.[249]

Finally, brothers, farewell. Be complete, comfort each other, strive to be of one mind, and live in peace——and the God of love and peace will be with you. Greet one another with a holy kiss. All the saints greet you. The grace of the Lord Jesus Christ, and the love of God, and the communion of the Holy Ghost, be with all of you. Amen.[250]

Men and brothers, though I have done nothing wrong against our people, or against the customs of our fathers, yet I was delivered as a prisoner from Jerusalem into the hands of the Romans. After they had examined me, they would have let me go because there was no reason for the sentence of death in my case. But because the Jews objected to this, I found it necessary to appeal to Caesar. This was not because I had any charge to level against my nation. For this reason, therefore, I called to see you, in order to speak with you——in that it is for the hope of Israel I am bound with this chain.[251]

I would to God, that not just you only, but also everyone who hears me this day, were almost like me, and altogether like me, except for these chains.[252]

I, Paul, write this salutation by my own hand. Remember my chains. Grace be with you. Amen.[253]

POSTSCRIPT

S tand upright on your feet.[254]
Let us go again and visit our brothers in every
city where we have preached the word of the Lord,
and see how they are doing.[255]

I command you in the name of Jesus Christ to come
out of her.[256]

Do yourself no harm, for we are all here.[257]

They have beaten us openly, uncondemned Romans
citizens, and have cast us into prison.

And now they want to throw us out secretly? Not at all.
Let them come themselves and escort us out personally.[258]

May I speak to you?[259]

Is it lawful for you to scourge a man who is a Roman,
and uncondemned?[260]

Yes.[261]

But I was born a free citizen.[262]

After I have been there, I must also see Rome.[263]

Do not be troubled in yourselves, for his life is in him.[264]

Men, I see that this voyage will end with much injury
and damage, not only of the cargo and ship, but also of
our lives.[265]

Men, you should have listened to me, and not set sail
from Crete, which brought about this damage and loss.
But now I encourage you to take heart——there will be

no loss of life with you, but only of the ship. For this last night an angel of God stood by me——a God whose I am, and whom I serve——saying, "Do not fear, Paul. You must be brought before Caesar, and behold, God has given you all those who sail with you. Therefore, men, take heart because I believe God, and it shall be just as I was told. But we must run aground on some island.[266]

Unless these men remain with the ship, you cannot be saved.[267]

This day marks the fourteenth day that you have waited without eating, having taken nothing. Therefore I urge you to take some food. It will strengthen you, and not a hair fall will fall from the head of any of you.[268]

I must by all means keep this feast that comes in Jerusalem, but I will return again to you, if God wills it.[269]

Have you received the Holy Ghost since you believed? . . . Into what were you baptized then? . . . John indeed baptized with the baptism of repentance, saying to the people that they should believe on the one who would come after him, that is, on Jesus Christ.[270]

What do you mean by weeping and breaking my heart? For I am ready, not merely to be bound, but also to die in Jerusalem for the name of the Lord Jesus.[271]

Men and brothers, I have lived with a clear conscience before God until this day.

God will strike you, you whitewashed wall. You sit there to judge me according to the law, and command me to be struck contrary to the law? And those who stood by said, "Do you revile God's high priest?" And so Paul said, "I did not know, brothers, that he was the high priest. For it is written, 'You shall not speak evil of a ruler of your people.'"

Men and brothers, I am a Pharisee, the son of a Pharisee. I have been brought here because of the hope and resurrection of the dead.[272]

Bring this young man to the chief captain. He has a certain thing to tell him.[273]

Inasmuch as I know that you have been a judge in this nation for many years, I am willing to answer for myself cheerfully. You may easily ascertain that it has only been twelve days since I went up to Jerusalem in order to worship. They did not find me in the temple disputing with anyone, neither was I raising a tumult——not in the synagogues, and not in the city. Neither can they prove the things they are now accusing me of.

But I do confess this to you——according to the way that they call a sect, in that way I worship the God of my fathers. I believe all things which are written in the law and in the prophets. And I have hope in God, which they themselves share, that there shall be a resurrection of the dead, both of the just and unjust. And I take particular pains to always have a conscience clear of offense toward God and men.

Now after many years I came to bring alms to my nation, along with offerings. That is when certain Jews from Asia found me in the temple, *purified*, and I was neither with a multitude, nor with a tumult. They ought to have been present here before you, in order to object, if they had anything against me. Or let these men here say what it is, if they have found any wrongdoing on my part while I appeared before their Council——unless it is for the fact that I cried out while standing among them that I was called before them because of the resurrection of the dead.[274]

I have not offended in anything at all——not against the law of the Jews, not against the temple, and not against Caesar.[275]

I stand at Caesar's judgment seat, where I ought to be judged. To the Jews I have done no wrong, as you yourself know very well. For if I am an offender, or have done anything worthy of death, I do not refuse to die. But unless they can accuse me of any of these things, no many can turn me over to them. I appeal to Caesar.[276]

NOTES

INTRODUCTION

i   Melanchthon, *Commentary on Romans* (1540), trans. Fred Kramer (St. Louis: Concordia, 1992).

ii Luther, *Commentary on Romans, Introduction*, trans. Andrew Thornton, "Vorrede auff die Epistel S. Paul: an die Romer," in *D. Martin Luther: Die gantze Heilige Schrifft Deudsch 1545 aufs new zuericht,* ed. Hans Volz and Heinz Blanke (Munich: Roger & Bernhard, 1972), 2:2254-2268.

iii Godet, *Commentary on Romans,* Introduction.

iv Calvin, *Commentary on Romans,* Introduction.

v   Tyndale, *Introduction to Romans.*

GRACE AND PEACE

1   Philem 1:1; Eph 1:1; Gal 1:1; Phil 1:2; Col 1:1; 1 Tim 1:1; 2 Tim 1:1; Titus 1:1; 1 Cor 1:1

2   Philem 1:1; 1 Tim 1:1; 2 Tim 1:1; 1 Cor 1:1; 2 Cor 1:1

3   Titus 1:1

4   2 Tim 1:1; 1 Cor 1:1; 2 Cor 1:1

5   Titus 1:1

6   1 Tim 1:1

7   2 Tim 1:1

8   Gal 1:1; 1 Cor 1:1, Rom 1:1

9   Eph 1:1; Col 1:1; Titus 1:1

10 Gal 1:1

11 Rom 1:1-4

12 Titus 1:2-3

13 1 Tim 2:7

14 Rom 1:5-6

15 Rom 1:7

16 2 Tim 1:2

17 1 Tim 1:2; 2 Tim 1:2. I know. This project requires a conflate letter to be addressed to Timothy and to be from him at the same time. Life is tough.

18 Titus 1:4

19 Gal 1:2

20 Col 1:2

21 Eph 1:1

22 1 Thess 1:1; 2 Thess 1:1

23 1 Cor 1:2; 2 Cor 1:2

24 1 Tim 1:2; Titus 1:4

25 Also Philem 1:3; also Eph 1:2; also Gal 1:3; Col 1:2; 1 Thess 1:1; 2 Thess 1:1; 1 Tim 1:2; 2 Tim 1:2; 1 Cor 1:3; 2 Cor 1:2; Rom 1:7

26 2 Tim 1:2

27 Titus 1:4

28 Gal 1:4-5

29 1 Thess 1:1; 2 Thess 1:1; 1 Cor 1:1; 2 Cor 1:1

30 Gal 1:2

31 Phil 1:1; Col 1:1

32 Philem 1:1

33 Phil 1:1

34 Philem 1:7

170 1 Cor 7:25-40. In the section about marrying or not marrying "his virgin," my understanding of this corresponds to the translation offered in the New English Bible, which is that Paul was addressing the odd custom of celibate marriages. The practice was nervously tolerated down to the Council of Elvira, when everybody was then told to knock it off.

171 1 Thess 4:1-8

172 1 Cor 7:8-16

AVOIDING WRANGLES

173 Rom 14:1-6

174 Phil 2:12-18

175 1 Cor 6:1-11

176 Titus 1:10-16

177 Rom 14:7-9

178 Gal 5:1-5

179 Rom 14:10-16

180 Gal 4:1-11

181 Rom 14:17-23

182 Col 2:16-23

A RIGHT USE OF LAW

183 1 Tim 1:3-11

184 1 Tim 4:1-11

185 1 Cor 6:12-20

186 2 Cor 7:1

187 1 Cor 8:1-13

188 1 Cor 10:23-11:1

FOOLS FOR CHRIST

189 1 Cor 4:1-21

190 1 Thess 4:9-12

MEN AND WOMEN

191 Rom 15:1-4

192 2 Tim 3:14-17

193 Rom 15:5-6

194 Eph 5:22-33

195 Col 3:18-25

196 1 Tim 2:8-15

197 1 Cor 7:1-7

198 1 Cor 11:2-16

WALKING WORTHY

199 Titus 2:1-10

200 Col 4:1

201 2 Thess 3:6-15

202 Rom 15:7-16

203 Phil 1:27-30

204 Rom 15:17-29

205 Col 4:2-6

206 1 Tim 4:12-5:16

207 2 Tim 4:1-8

208 Rom 15:30-33

209 1 Tim 5:23-25

FAREWELLS AND BENEDICTIONS

210 Rom 16:1-16

211 Col 4:7-17

212 Rom 16:17-19

213 Eph 6:10-20

214 Rom 16:20

215 2 Tim 2:1-7

216 Phil 4:10-20

217 1 Tim 6:17-19

218 Philem 1:23

219 Philem 1:21-22

POSTSCRIPT